Leading a Child to Independence

A Positive Approach to Raising Children Through the Teens

Leading a Child to Independence

A Positive Approach to Raising Children Through the Teens

PAUL & JEANNIE McKEAN
and Maggie Bruehl

Here's Life Publishers

Published by
HERE'S LIFE PUBLISHERS, INC.
P. O. Box 1576
San Bernardino, CA 92402

HLP Product No. 951459

Library of Congress Cataloging-in-Publication Data
McKean, Paul.
    Leading a child to independence.
    Bibliography: p.
    1. Child rearing — Religious aspects — Christianity.
2. Child development.   3. Autonomy in children.
4. Self-reliance in children.   I. McKean, Jeannie,
1941-   . II. Bruehl, Maggie, 1948-   . III. Title.
HQ769.3.M38   1986   649'.1   86-9858
ISBN 0-89840-144-5 (pbk.)

Unless otherwise indicated, all Scripture quotations are from the New American Standard Bible, © The Lockman Foundation, 1960, 1962, 1963, 1968, 1971, 1973, 1975, 1977, and are used by permission.

FOR MORE INFORMATION, WRITE:

L.I.F.E. — P.O. Box A399, Sydney South 2000, Australia
Campus Crusade for Christ of Canada — Box 300, Vancouver, B.C. V6C 2X3, Canada
Campus Crusade for Christ — 103 Friar Street, Reading RG1 1EP, Berkshire, England
Lay Institute for Evangelism — P.O. Box 8786, Auckland 3, New Zealand
Great Commission Movement of Nigeria — P.O. Box 500, Jos, Plateau State Nigeria, West Africa
Campus Crusade for Christ International — Arrowhead Springs, San Bernardino, CA 92414, U.S.A.

DEDICATION

To Tanya and Todd,
 Becky, Jessica, Jaime and Amanda,
  children we desire to be independent in the Lord,
   able to enjoy life confidently in an uncertain world.

CONTENTS

Foreword 9

Preface 11

Introduction 13

PART ONE -

    Chapter 1 - Panic in the Nest 15

    Chapter 2 - Others Who Have Flown the Coop . 19

    Chapter 3 - Determining a Flight Path 27

    Chapter 4 - Excuting the Perfect Takeoff 39

PART TWO -

    Chapter 5 - Spiritual Development 49

    Chapter 6 - Physical Development 67

    Chapter 7 - Intellectual Development 81

    Chapter 8 - Social Development 95

    Chapter 9 - Emotional Development 107

    Chapter 10 - Financial Development 121

PART THREE -

    Chapter 11 - Staying on Course 131

    Chapter 12 - How Does it Feel to Fly? 139

    Chapter 13 - Resources and Worksheets 151

FOREWORD

I am asked to read numerous manuscripts and books designed to assist parents in their tasks of rearing children. What a delight to find one which is truly practical, sensible, and indispensible! Too many couples today drift throughout the journey of marriage and parenthood with no direction or plans. This unique and much needed book will be a breath of fresh air to the reader. It is well organized and clearly written. Any parent will be able to implement this guide without feeling overwhelmed. The authors give a balanced directive for the development of all areas of a child's life. It is rich with suggestions and resources for parents at any stage and I would highly recommend this book for all prospective parents.

H. Norman Wright

PREFACE

Writing this book has been a challenge for all of us —
First of all, the simple logistics of coordinating two
husbands, six children ranging in age from zero to twenty,
full-time ministries and travel schedules have been unreal.
In the two years it has taken us to write this book we have
dealt with sprained ankles, broken bones, automobile acci-
dents, surgery, death in the family, pregnancy and childbirth,
twenty-one international tours and over seventy-five national
trips. Needless to say, it has been a growing experience.

Second, this book has presented a writing challenge.
Coordinating the input of three authors while writing in the
first person has stretched our creative thinking beyond sanity.
When we have reached a point of hopelessness, I've meshed
Paul's contributions into Jeannie's perspective and referred
to my family's experiences as "I have a friend who. . ."
Somewhere in the conglomeration I hope you get the picture
that the book was a joint effort.

Third, we have faced a spiritual challenge. Paul, Jeannie,
Roger and I are all painfully aware of our failures as parents.
Nowhere else does Satan accuse us more of hypercritical
living. But in spite of our faults, we feel God has taught
us lessons we can pass on to others. And we have done
some things right. So take what you can, learn from our
experiences, and let the Lord motivate you as you take up
the challenge of leading your children to independence — of
teaching them to fly.

MAGGIE BRUEHL

INTRODUCTION

The day I stepped on my college campus for the first time, I was anticipating meeting gals who were tops — maybe even one I might marry someday. I never dreamed then of the tremendous wife and family God would give me.

When Jeannie and I were married, we had some principles we thought would carry us through. The challenge of marriage and raising children seemed staggering at times, but we believed we had commitments which could make the difference between success and failure. To begin with, we were married for life — we would never threaten divorce, not even in joking. We would be transparent and talk out our differences as they happened. We would continue to treat each other as we did when we were dating. (I still open the car door for her.)

Our children, we believed, were gifts, and God expected us to exercise stewardship over them. Our end objective was that these children should be able to function in life as total and whole individuals, able to face life as independent, fulfilled people.

In this book we share the reflections, ideas, and struggles of a real family. We have our days, just like you do. When we held those little people in our arms, we determined we didn't want them just to grow up, like "Topsy." We wanted to establish principles for them and a plan by which we could guide their development.

Where would we start? We began by asking ourselves some questions: "What do we want our children to be like when they are eighteen and on their own? How will they conduct themselves when we're not around? How will they handle tough issues without our input?" Those were hard questions to answer. It is now more than twenty-five years since I set foot on that college campus, and the "girl of my dreams" *is* the girl of my dreams. My "little people" are now in college. I can't hold them bundled in my arms like I used to, although we still hug a lot. They grew up so fast we hardly realized it. They are my best friends. Our family is a special unit, now heading in several directions as our children pursue the dreams God has for them. It's hard to see them go, but we have confidence that Tanya and Todd have the background to be all God has created them to be.

In the pages of this book you will find our attempts to put together a family plan which, even with its imperfections, will spark thoughts of what you can do to bring your children along on a personal development path. It is a workbook of ideas. Choose the tools which best suit you and your situation. Our objective is to see children prepared to face a harsh world with confidence and dependence on the solid Rock, Jesus Christ and His Spirit, and to enable those children to live life to the fullest.

Join us in the exciting adventure of raising children! It's never too late to begin. Our trails were rarely perfect and our children know that better than anyone. However, beyond your frustrations and tears are those young men and women who someday will stand before you and love you for your desire to help them be independent.

PAUL MCKEAN

1

Panic in the Nest

They will mount up with wings like eagles, They will run
and not get tired, they will walk and not become weary.

Isaiah 40:31

It was one of those priceless days in June when serenity broke through our hectic schedule and my kids said, "Mom, let's go to the park!" I was ready. Tanya was ten, a serious age when everything seems important. She was hanging off the side of the swing set practicing gymnastics in a fantasy of the Olympics, while Todd, a more reckless eight, was defying the laws of gravity sliding up the slide instead of down. I couldn't help thinking what special children God had given Paul and me.

In the midst of my reflections, my mind began to wander to some disturbing things I had been reading in the newspapers, of teenage runaways and rebellion, of middle-class kids facing drug arrests, and of the lack of a sense of morality in general. Looking around the Christian community, I received little assurance that our children would be immune. As I tried to picture what they would be like at age eighteen,

15

I became aware of a sense of panic. How could I know that someday I wouldn't see Todd or Tanya's picture in the paper and experience heartache for them as well as myself? How could I prepare these precious children for the years to come? How could I lead them to the independence that arises from a solid dependence on God?

For the next few days, my mind seemed preoccupied with the fear of what was going to happen to my children. Everything I saw seemed to confirm the idea that the world was in chaos. Even my Bible gave no hope of the world getting better. Instead, it assured me that the decline of morality would accelerate until the day of Christ's return. There was a reality I knew I would have to face sooner or later.

But I didn't like this prospect. Although the horizon looked bleak, I fought the idea that my children were doomed. I could not see anywhere in God's Word that children had to rebel, that there had to be a generation gap, or that sin would overtake God's grace.

What I did find was that God is serious about how we raise our children. We have a responsibility as parents not to let rebellion run rampant. In the days of the Old Testament, rebellion itself was such a serious offense that parents were commanded to take their unruly children to the community to be punished, i.e., death by stoning. Of course, we don't promote such practices today, but it made sense that if we as parents would begin to take the raising of our children as seriously as God did in the Old Testament, as if their very lives depended on it, their lives and the world would be very different.

I also found that God did not want me to panic in raising the children or to become fatalistic. Verses like Joshua 1:9 encouraged me with "Be strong and courageous! Do not tremble or be dismayed, for the Lord your God is with you." Other verses encouraged me to depend on God for my strength and wisdom. I knew there had to be a solution.

I couldn't help thinking about the birds and what a seemingly effortless task they have in raising their little birdlings. The old saying, "Let nature take its course," somehow works better for birds than for humans. But as I thought further about the birds, I realized they have done more than singing in the trees and pulling out a few worms. Lovingly, the mama and papa birds built a nest in the safest place they could find. Then for weeks they nestled their little eggs beneath their bodies, resisting the temptations to do other things. After the eggs hatched the real work began with the endless effort of providing for their babies' needs, modeling what they had been taught, training their little ones until they were able to leave the nest and fend for themselves in a world full of cats and disease and hunger. Not an easy task! I realized I really wouldn't trade my life for a bird's life after all!

The analogies were obvious. Paul and I as parents had tried to provide a good environment in which to raise our children. We had been careful to buy a house with a yard big enough for a swing set. We had checked out schools and had located the YMCA and the best pediatrician in town. As hard as it was, when the children were babies, we gave them the constant attention they needed to keep them warm emotionally as well as physically, giving up some of our own desires just to "be with them." Later, as their capacities grew, it was all we could do to keep up with their activities without sacrificing our own. It seemed we were always going somewhere, doing something; and we knew the pace was not going to get slower as the children got older.

We wanted to raise children who some day would be able to fly away from the nest and, with the grandeur of eagles, soar into the future. We wanted them to be proud of themselves as individuals and have the confidence they would need to be successful in this world. We wanted them to know about "cats" and "hunters" and have the skills to escape. More than anything, we wanted them to be all God wanted them to be and to look to Him for their guidance.

But we did not have the instincts of the birds, nor was the environment our children were about to enter as simple as nature. We felt we needed to do more than we had been doing to see that Tanya and Todd would have the skills they would require to survive not only physically, but emotionally, spiritually, financially and intellectually as well. We needed a plan.

What you are about to read is a record of the encouragement and ideas the Lord gave us in order to bring our children to independence, to being "able to fly." The process is not completed, nor was it perfectly executed. But I will have to say that at twenty and eighteen our children are far more developed in every area of their lives than they would have been had we left the process to "nature."

Thought questions

How do you feel about raising your children?

What have you done to prepare them for independent living?

Knowing your children's strengths and weaknesses, what do you think they will be like when they grow up? (Think positively, then think negatively.)

2

Others Who Have Flown the Coop

Declaration of Independence

When in the Course of human events, it becomes necessary for one people to dissolve the political bands which have connected them with another, and to assume among the powers of the earth, the separate and equal station to which the Laws of Nature and of Nature's God entitle them, a decent respect to the opinions of mankind requires that they should declare the causes which impel them to the separation.

We hold these truths to be self-evident, that all men are created equal, that they are endowed by their Creator with certain unalienable Rights, that among these are Life, Liberty, and the pursuit of Happiness.

Independence — a word that inspires some to acts of courage and others to fearful trembling. I never really had thought about it, but after talking to others I became aware that independence can be a "red-letter" word, a flag word with strong emotional impact. Deep down in the hearts of many parents is the fear that independence will mean pain — pain of aloneness, separation, maybe even a tearing apart.

They have visions of a prideful, haughty child yelling, "I'll do it my own way!" and then slamming the door behind him.

But as I looked at the birds, I saw quite another picture. There were no birdlings saying, "I'll do it my way!" and bolting out of the nest before their time. Instead I saw nurturing and caring and even a gentle nudging by "Mom" and "Dad" to get the young ones going. I've even seen parents and birdlings fly away together.

After watching the children on the playground that day in June, I contemplated the difference between what I desired for my children and the horror stories I had heard about adolescence. I knew there had to be a better way to help my children mature. I didn't want to go through the pain of losing them; but at the same time, I didn't want to keep them dependent on us. I wanted them to grow and to be able to find their own way in the world.

As I thought about the word "independence," I realized why it had such a double meaning. For example, looking at independence from a political point of view, to the mother country it does mean separation and loss. But to the new nation it means freedom and equality. To both, independence can mean either mutually supportive relationships or continued conflict for generations. The deciding factor relates to how the independence is gained rather than the fact that it occurs.

Independence will come, in one form or another, as a child matures into an adult. If nothing else, our government will grant independence by right of age. Every individual has an inherent drive to experience his own will, and unless it is driven out by discouragement, that drive is the motivation for self-actualization. But at some point, the child will carry the responsibilities of driving a car, earning a livelihood, paying taxes, voting, and possibly defending the nation. He also decides his own spiritual fate. Parents may have a huge influence, but the choices remain with the developed child.

I found it helpful to think past my feelings about "independence" and look at the elements which make it such a powerful drive. I thought about the bold step our nation took in declaring its independence from the mother country, England. Little did those brave men in the secret room, laboring over quill and parchment, realize the significant philosophical statement they were making. Unknowingly they poured the concrete in which the foundation of one of the greatest nations of the world would be set — an act which later would inspire others towards national self-determination.

Those principles of independence are reflections of the same elements we experience as individuals within a nation. Independence is a right of the people — of a corporate group of people as well as of an individual. Over the centuries thousands have died to protect that right of independence.

A look back

By looking back at our own nation's Declaration of Independence, we parents can better understand the elements which go into the drive for independence. Our purpose here is not to make a complete analysis of the document, but to demonstrate ideals which reflect the thinking of men during the 1700s and continue to inspire men today.

First, independence is something which occurs "in the course of human events." As I said before, it is inevitable. Some parents live with the fantasy that their sons or daughters will never leave home, or that if they do leave, there will always be a type of umbilical cord joining children and parents. In fact, sometimes parents transfer this fantasy to their children, giving them the feeling that the parents will always provide for them emotionally and physically. As beautiful as the fantasy may feel, in reality it is devastating. It leaves emotionally crippled parents living their lives through emotionally crippled children who then feebly try to perform as adults while avoiding the responsibilities of determining the destiny of their country, offspring, and society. The results are a loss of independence for all — past, present and future.

Second, it becomes necessary "for one people to dissolve the political bands which have connected them with another."

There are two noteworthy elements in this statement. It tells us that "one people" is enough to break the bonds which held the two together; independence does not have to be the result of a consensus. Obviously there will be less conflict if all agree, but it only takes one to set the stage for independence. Parents may decide when the time has come, or the child may reach the conclusion he needs to experience his own rights as an individual. Whichever it is, each holds the power to determine when the separation will be declared.

It also states that "political bands" need to be broken. Independence does not necessarily mean all bands need to be broken. America was connected to England by ancestry, finances, loyalty, trade, political and religious philosophy, and in many other ways. If England had responded to us as they did years later to Canada's quest for independence, history would have to be rewritten. Instead of intense hatred and bitterness which resulted in conflict for the next fifty years, America could have enjoyed a supportive alliance. Handled correctly, independence within a family can dissolve bonds which inhibit a sense of individuality and personal dignity, while preserving those bonds which create a support system beneficial to all.

Third, independence is to "assume among the powers of the earth, the separate and equal station to which the Laws of Nature and of Nature's God entitle them." Again, there are two elements in this statement. Independence is a "separate and equal station," or position in life. Connection with a mother or a mother country is vitally important in the beginning stages, but with maturity comes the desire for separation and a sense of self-determination. A toddler needs the freedom to investigate flowers with funny looking bugs in them, but he also needs the security of mother when he gets stung. As he matures, he becomes wiser in his investigations; and if he does get stung, he learns to care for himself. He may even resent his mother's overprotection as he begins to sense his own separateness and equality.

The Declaration of Independence goes on to state the

endowment of independence is in the "Laws of Nature and of Nature's God." We cannot be sure of all the authors' individual beliefs, but it is interesting to note the universal admittance of a supreme being and the order of the universe guided by Him. Independence is not just a good ideal some men dreamed up, but our forefathers gave it divine credit as being from God. Certainly, as people investigate the teachings of Christ, a strong sense of individuality emerges as they are encouraged to make personal decisions in regard to their faith. Few dare to question the influence biblical Christianity has had in giving independence to slaves and rights to women and minority groups. As we parents consider independence, we need to recognize God as its source.

Fourth, we read, "a decent respect to the opinions of mankind requires that they should declare the causes which impel them to the separation." Nothing is more personal to one's identity than opinions; and in order for a person or a nation to have a sense of dignity or integrity, those opinions must be heard and respected. Obviously our nation felt strongly about the causes which impelled separation, and those causes needed to be clearly stated.

In families today, some of the reasons for separation sound more like excuses to me. I hear things like, "The house got too small," or, "They went away to college." In some cases the issues become so highly emotional that blame is placed on one person or the other: "I just couldn't live with her anymore," or "He was a lazy bum." Instead of making character judgments or situational excuses, we should realize a simple fact of life: it is time for the child confidently to take up responsibility as an equal among adults and to receive the respect due. The transition is smoother if everyone understands in concrete terms exactly what is happening and why. In the Declaration of Independence our founders took the time to list in detail their causes so there would be no misunderstanding as to why the separation was occurring. Had England been granting independence at her own initiative, she could have listed her reasons for feeling America had earned independence. Either way, recognizing honest reasons for separation eliminates misunderstandings.

Fifth, the writers of our Declaration felt all the above truths were "self-evident" — not some philosophy unique to a small group, but principles no one could or should deny. It seemed clear to them "that all men are created equal, that they are endowed by their Creator with certain unalienable Rights. . . ." These truths have been proved over the centuries; and when these rights are infringed upon, revolution occurs.

These rights include "Life, Liberty, and the pursuit of Happiness." We parents must keep these rights in mind as we grant independence to our children. It is the child's "Life," not ours. God was instrumental in using us in the creation and early training of the life, but ownership of the life is between the Creator and what He has created. We can love, protect, teach, correct and train to the best of our abilities, but the bottom line for the quality of life is up to the individual. In recognizing this, we gain a tremendous amount of freedom as well as a balance in responsibility. As parents our responsibility is to be obedient before the Lord in what we do and say, but the final results are between the individual and God. This also applies to an individual's decision to trust Jesus Christ and receive not only an "abundant life" here on earth,[1] but also the right to have "eternal life."[2]

The right of "Liberty" implies freedom from the rules or regulations of another. While in the parents' home, the child is under the rules of the household. When he becomes independent, he should have the right to determine his own rules for his life and future household. Often these rules are very similar to the parents' because values are the same, but it is important for the individual to sense that the rules are of his own initiative and not imposed by someone else. The difference is similar to that between compliance through fear and compliance through personal integrity — for instance, the difference between obeying the speed limit because of the presence of a police officer and obeying because of a belief that the law is just and worth obeying.

The "pursuit of Happiness" is another right. It includes the rights of self-actualization and self-determination. We laugh at stories of a father giving his three-day-old son a baseball glove, but it's not so funny when we see a grown man pressured into a business or a career in which he has no interest. Every person has the right to determine and pursue his or her own value of happiness. After all, who can sense the feeling of happiness except the individual? Yet somehow parents seem tempted to feel they know what would make their children happy. They lament, "If only he had married so-and-so," or "I could have set him up with money." We need to realize that true happiness comes from more than a job or a mate; it comes from within the individual. Each of us is responsible for his or her own happiness.

A look within

As Paul and I looked at our typical American family, we did not want a "revolutionary war" in our household. Just as England had been the "parent" country nurturing, financing, protecting her territory, we had been nurturing, protecting, supporting our children. But the time came when the American patriots needed to be heard without discrimination, able to determine their own destiny. When this equality was not granted freely, a painful, violent separation erupted.

I'm sorry to say that revolutionary war does occur within families of America, families who hold dear the American view of independence. When it comes to letting children go so they can enter the world as independent adults, parents sometimes err either on the side of caring too much, so that loss and fear cloud rational thinking, or of not caring enough to prepare the children adequately for their new responsibilities. Parental actions range from the extreme of giving independence casually, too early, to waiting so long that the child comes to a point of active rebellion.

Paul and I love our children, and we wanted a lifetime of mutually supportive relationships. We knew we needed to teach the children what they needed to know in order to be independent. But as we looked around, we wondered if we were expecting the impossible. Instead of finding other more experienced parents to model, we sensed confusion, frustration and desperation.

The reality of independence hit us. It was easy to see why America and England went to war: England refused to let go and the colonies refused to stay dependent. Like many parents, little by little, England grew weary with the struggle. She surrendered and reluctantly gave the colonies their freedom.

Deep inside, we still believed independence did not have to mean warfare, and God's Word seemed to confirm our belief. The Bible never promised the teenage years had to be a bloody revolution. Instead, we were promised an abundant life provided through Jesus Christ.[3] Instead of frustration, we were promised peace.[4] And instead of desperation, we were promised hope.[5] Together Paul and I claimed these promises not only for our lives, but for the lives of our children.

By the way, thinking back to the analogy of the birds, it's interesting to note that the national symbol of our country is an eagle with his wings spread ready to soar.

Thought questions

How do you feel about your children being "independent"?

What points in the comparison of America's "Declaration of Independence" to a child's independence impressed you the most? Why?

Where do you struggle the most in thinking about granting independence to your child?

3

Determining a Flight Path

It isn't the gale, but the set of my sail that determines
the course of my life.

Ron Dunn

So where do you start when you want to raise children
who are independent? As I looked at my children playing,
I knew Paul and I had a hard job ahead of us; but more
than ever before, I realized it was necessary. We were
fortunate to have some free time coming up in our schedule,
so we earmarked it to spend deciding what directions we
would take in helping our children become confident about
meeting the world around them.

For some time my husband and I had been familiar with
making goals for our own lives; so it seemed natural to
think about goals for our children's development. We began
by trying to envision what we felt we wanted them to be
like at age eighteen, the legal age when the government
considers them "adults." In the process we made a list of
things we thought they should know. We covered almost
everything — how to cook, budget, fix a flat tire, find

verses in the Bible, etc. We listed books they should read
and housekeeping skills they needed to know. It seemed
equally important to us that Tanya know basic mechanics
and that Todd have a working knowledge of a kitchen.
Trying to not limit ourselves by traditional roles, we systemat-
ically went through six different categories (financial,
spiritual, social, physical, emotional, intellectual) thinking
each through and getting a feel for what the children would
need to know.

We did want to be careful, in the development process,
not to predetermine our children's personalities, character
traits or personal preferences. As we mentioned in Chapter
2, they did have the rights of "Life, Liberty, and the pursuit
of Happiness" and we didn't want to take away any of
those. Todd needed to know how to cook, but whether he
became a gourmet chef or a Big Mac addict was his own
choice. We still needed to give him the basic skills. He
didn't even have to enjoy cooking, but he needed to be
equipped in order to make choices freely and not out of
lack of ability. We wanted to give the children the foundations
from which to build without limiting their opportunity for
personal expression.

As we got started, Paul and I realized three things. First,
working up such a detailed plan for the development of our
children would take a lot of time and energy. As I looked
at those two young bodies and then imagined them as adults,
I felt assured the time and effort we spent would be multiplied
over and over again in their quality of life. Second, we
realized how inadequate we were to take on this job. Apart
from the guidance of the Holy Spirit, it was impossible.
Third, we realized the job had to begin with us. We needed
to develop our communication and oneness as a couple in
order to be consistent models for the children.

So we developed what we called "planning weekends"
in order to give ourselves the quality of time we needed to
seek the Lord, to grow ourselves and to develop a plan. We
looked for a neutral place away from work and home where
both of us could be free to evaluate our lives and our chil-

dren's lives without the distractions of daily living. Besides relaxing, we took an objective look at where we had been, where we were going, and what we would still like to see happen. We tried to find environments where we could feel unthreatened and free to dream our dreams.

Personal planning

On our first planning weekend, we took with us questions someone suggested we discuss regarding communication and personal growth. Before tackling the job of teaching our children, we needed to solidify the atmosphere in our home to make a fertile field for our children's growth. We also recognized our need for better communication just to work out our basic plan. We agreed we had to be honest and vulnerable with each other as we talked through crucial issues such as:

Do you feel your mate listens to what you say?

Does your mate have a tendency to say things which would better be left unsaid?

Is it sometimes difficult to understand your mate's feelings?

What would make understanding easier?

Does your mate try to lift your feelings when you're down or depressed? Does it help? Why or why not?

When a problem arises which needs to be resolved, do you feel you and your mate are able to discuss it together? If not, what hinders you?

Do you and your mate engage in individual interests?

Do you and your mate enjoy common interests other than the home and children?

Do you and your mate take time to relax and dream together?

Including the children

After working on our own communication, we looked at how our children fit into our personal plans. We saw that in reality we would have our children for only eighteen years out of the ninety-five years we planned to live. This meant only one-fifth of our lives would be centered around the children. However, we saw this one-fifth section as the greatest responsibility of our entire lives. As a result we needed to ask ourselves some honest questions about how the part would fit into the whole:

What do we as a couple want for our lives? What do we feel our purpose is before God?

How do the children fit into our purpose?

In light of our personal desires, work, church and social responsibilities, what kind of priority should the children be given?

How do we fit the priority of our children into our already over-extended schedules?

As we considered our purpose before the Lord, Paul and I felt it could be best summed up in Colossians 1:28,29: "And we proclaim Him, admonishing every man and teaching every man with all wisdom, that we may present every man complete in Christ. And for this purpose also I labor, striving according to His power, which mightily works within us." As a couple we wanted to proclaim Christ, admonishing and teaching others, including our children, in order to present them to the Lord. This verse was especially meaningful because it not only presented the purpose for our lives, but also the power we had through Christ.

Another verse which defined our purpose was Matthew 28:19: "Go ye therefore and make disciples of all the nations, baptizing them in the name of the Father and the Son and the Holy Spirit, teaching them to observe all things I commanded you, and lo, I am with you always, even to the end of the age." This verse also emphasized winning people to Christ and teaching them to follow Him. It ended with the promise that He would be with us as we were obedient to His Word.

So how did children fit into our purpose before God? First of all, it was obvious to us they were our number-one disciples. God had given these special ones to us to pour our lives into not just an hour once a week, but twenty-four hours a day, every day. We had the opportunity to help them, admonish them, teach them, from every area of our lives to every area of theirs.

So what kind of priority were we going to give our children in our lives? Mark 12 told us we were to love the Lord our God with all our heart, soul and mind, and to "love thy neighbor as thyself."[1] We realized our closest neighbors were our family; the children were to take priority in our lives before our work, friends, social life and even church activities.

Even though we had a hard time visualizing how changes could be made in our lifestyle, we knew it was an area in which we needed to make a commitment. As an act of our will, we committed ourselves to work week by week, looking at our schedules, deciding where we could include our children as our priority. We knew the patterns we set in the beginning would be major factors in all our lives in the future.

As I mentioned before, Tanya was ten and Todd eight when we started this process. We were facing at least ten years of commitment to our children. Of course, in some ways we would be committed to them for the rest of our lives; but we felt that complete responsibility toward them would end as they went to college or followed some other career path.

The next part of our planning included an evaluation of our children individually to see where they were in their development at that particular time. We asked ourselves two questions: (1) What are their strengths and weaknesses? and (2) How do they need to be developed? As I mentioned before, we viewed them from the vantage point of six areas of development: spiritual, physical, intellectual, social, emotional and financial.

Evaluative planning . . . spiritually

The first area was spiritual development. We listed the children's strengths and weaknesses as well as their spiritual interests. We asked ourselves such questions as:

What are the children's feelings toward church?

What is their personal commitment to Jesus Christ?

Do they have a biblical foundation for basic principles of living?

Do they understand the Spirit-filled life? Do they consistently walk in the Spirit?

What is their prayer life like?

What is their concern for non-Christian friends?

As we honestly looked at Tanya and Todd's spiritual
development, we also looked at our responsibility toward
them. Deuteronomy 6:7 reminded us that in teaching spiritual
principles, "You shall teach them diligently to your sons
and shall talk of them when you sit in your house and when
you walk by the way, when you lie down and when you
rise up." Teaching spiritual principles is a way-of-life experience, not a Sunday school exercise. Spiritual principles must
be a part of our children's lives. There is a place for specific
instruction, but there is also a place for consistent demonstration. We demonstrate spiritual principles, positive and
negative, through our daily walk with God.

But Paul and I also realized we needed a balance in our
view of our responsibility. We could teach our children
spiritual principles and strive to live them out before them,
but it was God's responsibility to bring these principles
home to their hearts. After all, each child has to have his
own personal relationship with God. We knew of situations
where children had grown up respecting the God of their
parents but never truly experienced a vital relationship with
God themselves. Isaiah 54:13, 17b, promised us, "And all
your sons will be taught (discipled) of the Lord, and the
well-being of your sons will be great. . . . This is the heritage of the servants of the Lord." We felt the seriousness of
our responsibility in teaching and modeling to our children
what God's Word had to say about developing their spiritual
lives. It was God's responsibility to work in their lives to
the extent they would allow Him.

Evaluative planning . . . physically

The next area for evaluation was physical. As all areas
of development are intertwined, obviously a spiritually aware
soul or a brilliant mind would be seriously handicapped if
housed in a feeble body. We asked ourselves some questions
about our children, such as:

Are they growing physically at a normal rate?

Are they healthy, or do they suffer from an abnormal amount of illness?

Are they physically attractive? Do they look healthy?

How coordinated are they?

Do they participate in sports? Are they able to support the team and compete for personal excellence?

Do they make wise choices in eating the right foods?

Are they aware of principles of cleanliness?

Do they have a good understanding of sexual growth and changes?

As we looked at God's Word, we were amazed at the emphasis it places on the physical aspect of our lives. Major Bible characters such as Samuel, Saul, David, Jesus and many others have reference made to their "stature," [2] whether they were called to physical responsibilities such as the military or to more intellectual or spiritual endeavors. In the New Testament, we saw an emphasis in Jesus' ministry on healing and feeding others, meeting physical as well as spiritual needs. The same emphasis was reflected in the disciples' ministry as they continued to carry out Christ's teachings. God's Word assures us, in chapters like Psalm 23, that the Lord will meet all our needs.

Evaluative planning . . . intellectually

Diogenes said, "The only good is knowledge and the only evil is ignorance." As we evaluated the intellectual area, we felt our responsibility was to give our children the information they would need to be responsible adults. But we were also aware of an important distinction. It is not solely knowledge or ignorance which is good or evil, but the application of them that leads to good or evil. We didn't want to develop individuals with brains but without hearts. One cannot separate the intellectual and the spiritual. We all have heard examples of computer experts who use their knowledge to embezzle funds or construction workers who use sub-standard materials; in both cases people use their knowledge for evil.

The Bible shows us that knowledge without spiritual wisdom is foolishness.[3] If we wanted to raise well-rounded children, we needed not only to teach them information but also to give them wisdom in how to use it. We wanted to develop our children's intellects to the fullest while at the same time building their wisdom. With that goal in mind, we looked at the children's development and asked ourselves questions like:

Are they curious about and interested in the world around them?

Are they excited about learning? Have they caught the idea that learning is fun? Do they have positive or negative feelings about learning?

How are their communication skills developing? Are they able to communicate exactly what they mean?

Are they achieving in school? Are their strengths and weaknesses in conceptual areas or in memorization?

Do they appreciate music and the arts?

Do they sense a relationship between what they learn and how they live?

Are they able to apply what they have learned?

Proverbs 2 reminds us, "For the Lord gives wisdom; From His mouth come knowledge and understanding."[4] It also promises, "For wisdom will enter your heart, And knowledge will be pleasant to your soul; Discretion will guard you, Understanding will watch over you to deliver you from the way of evil."[5] The Lord has created a beautiful, complex world as a reflection of who He is. Romans 1:20 says, "For since the creation of the world His invisible attributes, His eternal power and divine nature, have been clearly seen, being understood through what has been made. . . ." We wanted our children to know as much as they could about their world and the God who created it.

Evaluative planning . . . socially

As the saying goes, "No man is an island"; and in this fast-paced multi-relational world, we wanted our children to grow up with balanced social lives. We wanted them to be liked and yet to have the social skills to disagree tactfully when necessary. We also wanted them to feel confident in new situations. Since basic relationships and social skills begin at home, we asked ourselves questions such as:

How is their communication at home? Do they express themselves freely, yet with sensitivity?

Are they obedient and responsive to correction?

Do they creatively seek out ways to be helpful to their parents? To other siblings?

What are their responses to their sex roles?

Do they seem secure in their own identities?

After looking at our children's relationships at home, we then evaluated their relationships outside the home with questions like:

What are their relationships with their peers? Does each have many friends or just one or two?

What are the levels of their relationships? Are they close, too close, or do they just "hang around together"?

Do they show appreciation of others? Are they creative in showing their appreciation?

Do they have relationships in a wide age span? Are they able to relate to adults and children as well as peers?

Are they respectful of authority figures?

Do they have a tolerance of "different" people?

How do they relate to non-Christians? Do they have both Christian and non-Christian friends?

What are their manners like? Do they clearly understand why manners are important?

What are their responses to peer pressure?

Luke 2:52 reminds us that "Jesus kept increasing in wisdom and stature, and in favor with God and men." Being "in favor" with men is important to our lives and to our Christian witness. Paul encouraged Timothy to pick only men who had "a good reputation with those outside the church" for church leadership.[6] Jesus exhorted His disciples, "By this all men will know that you are my disciples, if you have love for one another."[7] Having love and respect for individuals reflects God's love and respect for us as individuals. Our children needed the personal gratification and assurance that they were able not only to function in society, but to add to it.

Evaluative planning . . . emotionally

How we feel and who we are are inseparable; our emotions are the grid through which we view life's experiences. At times emotions are our motivator and at times our discourager. We felt that the emotional area, although hard to evaluate because of its subjectivity, was one of the important areas needed to equip our children. We asked ourselves questions such as:

How are our children doing in the area of self-image?

What are their general dispositions? Do they experience extremes in their emotions?

Are they easy to get along with?

Are they adaptable to new situations?

How do they handle fear? Depression?

What is their basis for honesty?

Does each have a strong sense of personal integrity?

The Bible gives us our example in emotions. Because "God so loved the world," He sent us His son.[8] And it "grieved His heart" to see man's sin in Noah's day.[9] We seldom think about the emotions of God, but the Bible is full of illustrations regarding how He and others felt. We were aware that denied emotions could work havoc in a life. We wanted our children to feel life to its fullest and then to be able to channel those feelings toward positive effects.

Evaluative planning . . . financially

The last area of development we examined was financial. Our children had had little experience financially, and we were aware they needed more experience in the basics of money management. We asked ourselves questions such as:

Do they know how to count money?

Do they know how to use their money?

Do they know which kinds of purchases are wise and which are not?

Do they know how to set up and use a budget?

Do they know how to save? Do they have savings accounts?

Do they know how to work in order to earn money? Have they worked on jobs in the home? Have they worked for others?

Do they know what it means to give God one-tenth of their money? Do they know why they should give God one-tenth of their money?

Are they generous to others? Do they know the joy of giving?

Contrary to popular belief, the Bible has much to say about finances, and it does not say that "money is the root of all evil."[10] It is true that the love of money corrupts,[11] but the love of anything to excess is sin.[12] In order to teach our children not to love money, we felt we needed to show them realistically what money could and could not do. They needed to recognize that "the laborer is worthy of his wages"[13] in God's eyes. There is nothing to be ashamed of in hard work. They also needed to know that God says, "He who is faithful in a very little thing is faithful also in much, and he who is unrighteous in a very little thing is unrighteous also in much."[14] Handling the resources God has given us, both in our ability to work and in the use of our money, is important.

Looking back

Looking back, we can think of other questions we could have asked as we took stock of our position. The important thing was for us to view ourselves and the children candidly in relationship to where we wanted to go toward independence. Only after we knew where we were and could visualize where we wanted to be could we determine the steps necessary to get us there.

Thought questions

When can you make the time to establish a plan for your child? Think through and discuss the planning and evaluation questions in this chapter.

4

Executing the Perfect Takeoff

I sought the LORD, and He answered me,
And delivered me from all my fears.
They looked to Him and were radiant,
And their faces shall never be ashamed.

Psalm 34:4,5

After evaluating where we were and where the children
were, Paul and I saw we needed a plan to carry us from
the real to the ideal. Here were two children who had a lot
to learn, being tutored by two adults who felt totally unpre-
pared for the job. But as we analyzed our situation, we
began to see we had more resources than we originally
thought.

Most of our resources were subconscious. For example,
my friend's seven-year-old boy cut himself yesterday. His
mother immediately assessed the situation, evaluating how
much blood he was losing, how dirty the wound was, how
deep the cut ran, and what serious danger, if any, was
involved. She did all this amid the boy's hysterical screaming.
Then she brought to bear the resources which could help,
i.e., pressure, soap and water, antiseptic, and bandages.

Had it been necessary, she would have called a doctor to stitch the wound. Now I don't know who sat down and taught her all of that procedure, but somehow she learned it. The trick will be passing on her knowledge to her son, so when he is older and on his own he will know how to assess his own hurts and bring resources to bear on them.

The same is true of emotional hurts. I can remember when Tanya was in seventh grade and we had just moved to Florida. There were twin girls living up the block who, in Tanya's eyes, had everything — beautiful clothes, beautiful eyes, curly blonde hair and boyfriends. One morning at the bus stop they started teasing Tanya, saying she'd never have a boyfriend because she was such a "tomboy." Tanya was active in sports and loved physical activity; but these words had such a bite to them, her spirit was totally crushed. She and I spent a lot of time together the next few weeks. She needed me to hold her both physically and emotionally, and she needed to know I unconditionally loved her. Not only did I love her, but so did many others. Most of all, she needed to know God loved her and she had value in His eyes. Little by little the hurt healed, and her social calendar today proves how wrong those girls were. More important, Tanya learned a valuable lesson: Her worth should not be based on the opinions of others. Instead, the only opinions which really count are God's opinion of her and her opinion of herself. Now when she runs into similar situations she has the resources with which to deal with them.

So, through our evaluation, we saw a need to get some of these basic concepts out of our heads and into Todd's and Tanya's. The following chapters give examples of the elements we felt were important for the children to know. In no way do we feel the lists are complete. In fact, were we starting from scratch again, I know some factors would be different. That's what makes raising children such an adventure! No two children are alike, no two sets of parents are alike, and each child is being prepared for a unique position in life's circumstances. This is what makes our reliance on God vital!

In mountain climbing, one of the first things you do when facing the side of a cliff is to look for and develop toeholds. As Paul and I looked at the overwhelming job of raising our children, we felt our toeholds had to be in the Solid Rock, our LORD Jesus Christ. Many verses through the years have given us encouragement and stability, but one that has been especially secure is 1 Chronicles 28:8: "Observe and seek after all the commandments of the Lord your God in order that you may possess the good land and bequeath it to your sons after you forever." Joshua 1:9 helped us deal with our fear by encouraging us to "Be strong and courageous! Do not tremble or be dismayed, for the Lord your God is with you wherever you go."

Dangling on the side of the cliff with our toes gripping their toeholds, we realized we needed two more things. We already had envisioned our goal of standing on the mountaintop viewing our "independent" children, and through evaluation we had a good idea of where we were starting from. But from that point on the rock we realized we also needed focus and a plan.

When clinging to sheer rock, with the face of the cliff looking so broad, a climber can be overwhelmed by the thought of scaling it. He needs a plan for getting from the bottom to the top with the least amount of effort. Then he needs to focus on each step as he proceeds in logical order. If he meanders from side to side, he may enjoy the scenery; but he'll run out of time and energy before he gets to the top. Paul and I called the technique that helped us to both focus and plan, "action points."

Action points

Looking at the goal before us, we mapped out the steps we thought the children needed to take to get from where they were to where they should be — not only independent, but excited and confident about life. In some cases we could take what seemed to come naturally to us and transfer it into activities we taught our children. In other situations we realized we needed to gain new skills in order to give the children the background they needed.

In the area of spiritual development, we wanted our children, then eight and ten years old, to be consistent in spending quiet time with the Lord. In setting up action points for this, we felt the children needed:

(1) to know how to have a special time with the Lord;
(2) to have resources for in-depth study and know how to use them;
(3) to have personal convictions about why a quiet time is important;
(4) to develop a plan, by choosing a time and place for quiet time, and to put this plan into action;
(5) to evaluate their own quiet time periodically for quality and variety, and to make necessary adjustments.

In the area of physical development, we felt the children should know and use basic hygiene. But for our own benefit we needed to break down exactly what is meant by personal care and communicate it to the children. Our action points included:

(1) knowing what "hygiene" is;
(2) knowing why hygiene is important;
(3) knowing the resources available and how to use them (i.e., shampoo, conditioner, toothpaste, etc.);
(4) developing routines which would grow into good habits.

As we looked at each of the six areas of development, we felt that although each child had different needs, there were some basic skills each should have. Some children, because of their personalities or previous experience, know more than others. Therefore parents must assess each child, without relying on assumptions, and discover where to begin in their action points. If a child is a teen or pre-teen, the action points may be more advanced than for a younger child who needs to review the basics. I know one mother who tactfully taught her thirteen-year-old daughter how to wash her face when she seemed to be having a hard time with blemishes. It is easy to make assumptions as to what children should know by certain ages, but it's important to look at what they actually do know and practice daily.

Action points are the steps to the final product, the breakdown of all the elements which make the whole. They will differ with different children or parents. Breaking the goals into action points not only gives a general plan, but helps focus attention on important aspects of development.

Possibly you, as a parent, may be thinking, "I don't even know all this stuff!" I know Paul and I had our doubts. We had to research some areas in which we were weak, investing a certain amount of reflection as well as study. We really would encourage you to use the references in Chapter 13 as resources. One of the fears of parents is that they will leave in their children the same holes that riddle themselves. Since we have had a plan, we have been able to see a few of our holes stopped up. This is not to say we have "arrived," but we do feel that our children are better prepared to meet life than we were.

Communication is a key

Obviously, the way in which parents communicate a new plan of action is vital. It can be presented in a positive or negative manner, and the child's ability to receive and accept the plan will be just as positive or negative as its presentation. The idea that "attitudes are caught and not taught" is as true in this setting as any other in life.

Your children need to see your excitement about their potential. Self-image is a major stumbling block today of teenagers as well as adults. If you present your plan as "how to build your self-esteem" rather than "how to keep from failing," your children will receive it as such. They need to see that because they are so valuable to you and to God, you care enough to give them the best.

When Paul and I first communicated our plan to our children, we took them away for a special weekend. Paul had a fishing trip planned with some of the men he worked with, so he invited Todd along. Todd's little face lit up when he was invited to go fishing with "the men." While on this trip Paul and Todd took some time to be alone together. There, in the back country of Florida, Paul told Todd how proud he was of the way Todd was maturing and how he was looking forward to the day when Todd, confident of his abilities to relate to the world around him, would take the leadership of his own family. Paul presented the concept of an "earned independence" as a way to insure that Todd would have the skills he needed before he went to college.

In the meantime, Tanya and I took a "ladies' weekend out" at Disney World. We stayed in a motel and went shopping at Fiesta Village. She was beginning to choose her own clothes, and we had a fun time trying on all sorts of fancy fashions. That night, after dinner on the riverboat, we talked about how she was developing into her own person. In the next few years she would undergo many changes covering every area of her life. I told her that I wanted to do all I could to help her become confident of who she was and that there were some things her father and I felt she needed to know before she was out on her own. I let her choose which areas she wanted to start with and she chose the physical and intellectual. She became very excited as she realized she could do something tangible to become "grown up."

The child must know that he or she is important and valuable — that you are not setting up a standard for perfection but offering a direction in which to grow. The parents' communication of both of these principles is as essential as the information itself. If parents communicate negatively, they can destroy what they intended to build.

Timing

Our goal was to have each of our children independent by the middle of his or her senior year. As we looked around, it seemed to us that most teenagers first experienced independence when they left home for college or work. Up until then, they were basically under the responsibility of their parents.

But as we considered independence for our own children, we saw a problem. When should a child become responsible for himself? If children do not become responsible for themselves until out from beneath the parents' roof, where will they go when they have a problem to discuss or a

We all would like to think our children would call home at such times, but the truth of the matter is they probably will go to someone who is more convenient: a roommate, boyfriend, girlfriend or fellow employee. It may be a simple matter of accessibility, or they may go to others because they feel safer away from the emotional involvements that seem to go along with parents. Often parents revert back into authoritative roles when asked for advice, and assume responsibilitiy for the situation (after all, they had the responsibility for eighteen years!) instead of offering the support a young adult needs. Sometimes the young adult fears his parents will feel he's failing, will lose respect for him, and possibly will withdraw some phase of the newly granted independence.

The fact is, young adults will talk to someone. Instead of talking to parents, to whom they feel they must prove themselves, they probably will talk to peers. As they share what is often a mixture of combined ignorance and wishful optimism, they at least feel safe from the risks of judgment or authoritarianism.

Paul and I wanted to protect the open lines of communication we had worked so hard to build. We did not necessarily need to be the only voices our children considered, but we wanted to continue to have input in their lives during the tender period of newly-found independence. We wanted to know who else they were listening to and what advice was influencing their decisions. We also felt they needed a biblical perspective in making their decisions.

We felt that when we finished, our children should have a working knowledge of the elements of independence and should receive a formal or informal Declaration of Independence. Let me stress that this is an earned honor, not one given just because the child has hit a magic age. The world seems to tell children that if they can just manage to survive until age eighteen, they automatically achieve "maturity." Earned independence gives a young adult the satisfaction of knowing he or she has truly achieved the goal and has the basic tools with which to live and make decisions.

The beauty of giving an earned independence during or before the senior year is that the young adults are still in the home. In our family, we have agreed to cover room and board as long as the children are saving for college. Beyond this point, they are to be completely independent.

We define "completely independent" as having equal rights and responsibilities as adults in the household. It does not mean having the right to be inconsiderate of other family members. In any living situation, the rights of others have to be respected; and children need to learn this before receiving their independence. There is a subtle difference between children asking their parents for permission to go somewhere, and telling their parents they are going somewhere and coordinating this activity with the activities of others. It's like telling a friend you are going to the store and asking if you can get something for him. This kind of relationship should exist between mates, roommates, and friends.

As the child experiences independence from the shelter of home, open and honest communication should continue. The instruction in right and wrong is replaced by personal opinion in this period of letting go and taking on, all accomplished in an atmosphere of acceptance.

Implications

We have to admit we were overwhelmed as we looked at everything we wanted our children to know by the time they were halfway through their senior year. The time seemed so short and the list so terribly long. But as we took each section and worked from where they were to where we wanted them to be, we saw the task was not impossible. And, by the grace of God, we recognized our responsibility to encourage and direct our children in their growth.

The next few chapters contain some of the elements we saw as important in teaching our children to be independent. The list certainly is not complete. We want to encourage you to use it not as an authority, but as a jumping-off point to develop your own criteria uniquely fitting your child and your standards. Don't be discouraged if you're not able to accomplish every little detail of your plan. Instead, just realize that whatever you do in this direction will encourage development in your child which probably would not occur by happenstance. Your child is unique, and you are unique parents, and the Lord understands that. I'm so glad He doesn't require me to meet the standards of others but is just thrilled to see *me* grow. It will be helpful if you have that same spirit as you and your children grow. Then, stand back and watch them fly!

Thought questions

What is your vision for your child at age eighteen?

How do you plan to communicate your ideas about independence to your child?

What do you see as the benefits of an "earned" independence?

5

Spiritual Development

Spiritual:
— of or pertaining to God or to the soul as acted upon by
the Holy Spirit.

> Webster's New World Dictionary

— things that have their origin with God and which therefore
are in harmony with His character.

> An Expository Dictionary of New Testament Words

The first area we considered in the development of our
children was spiritual because as my husband Paul commented, "It is the center of all we are and all we are to
become." Without the Lord there is nothing — no real hope,
satisfaction or completion. We could train the children in
all the basics of living; but without the Lord as the center,
their lives would join others who have gone before them,
successful in the ways of men but empty and meaningless
in light of eternity. If we wanted our children's lives to
count not only in personal happiness but in multiplied joy
in the lives of others, we needed to concentrate on the one
area which would make them whole. As Colossians 1:16,17
tells us, "All things have been created through Him and for

Him. And He is before all things, and in Him all things hold together."

The reality of the spiritual importance of life was dramatically brought home to us last August as Paul and I were driving in the San Bernardino Mountains. A young woman in the car directly in front of us suddenly swerved across the road into oncoming traffic. We narrowly missed going off the cliff trying to avoid her car. As we got out to see if we could help, we came face to face with a scene neither of us can wipe from our memories. The accident involved seven people — the girl in the Subaru and six others in a van coming home from a youth retreat. In the car behind us was the girl's fiancé; they were to be married in ten days. She was a beautiful girl, a model, twenty-one years old, with a lifetime to look forward to. But as we took her out of her car, it was obvious she would never see that lifetime. Amid cries from her boyfriend to "do something," a doctor present told us there was nothing we could do. She was dead.

As a helicopter flew people out, Paul and I not only were sobered personally about life and death, but we suddenly realized that our children, who we hoped would have long lives of independence, growth, happiness, and security, might themselves never see the lives we anticipated. Every time I pass the bloodstained scar on that road, I am aware of the brevity of life and the suddenness of death, and feel more than ever the urgency of building into Tanya and Todd the principles of eternal value.

I have to admit it is easier to teach children the more functional areas of life than the spiritual — easier to show them how to wash clothes than to walk in the Spirit. I guess it's because in functional areas we enjoy a certain amount of expertise; but when we look at the spiritual, Paul and I are painfully aware we have not in any way "arrived" in our walks with God. We have had to keep in mind that our lack of ability in no way reflects the importance of the spiritual life. The only area of development the children can take with them is the spiritual, which offers them an "abundant life" not only here and now but for all eternity.[1] Even though we had not "arrived," it was vital to their lives that we teach them, demonstrate to them, and confess before them the joys and failures which come from a walk with the Lord.

Chapter 13 contains a list of elements we felt were important for our children to have in their relationship with the Lord. But before you skip to the end of the book, we want to explain what we meant in each of the elements and how we worked them through with the children. I have to smile as I remember the saying, "He was so heavenly minded, he was no earthly good." I'm sure you would agree with us that the truth of the spiritual life is fleshed out through daily living. We did not want children who simply could recite verses, but ones who had convictions deeply etched in their own personal experiences.

Knows how to study the Word of God

Physically, a man who cannot feed himself will have trouble surviving. Every child needs to learn how to get a spoonful of cereal into his mouth despite the mess he makes along the way. Yet I shudder as I think of the people I've come across who have been Christians for years but are still stumbling around trying to find the books of the Bible or are embarrassed to share personally what a verse means to them.

We wanted our children to be healthy in the Lord, which meant we needed to teach them how to feed themselves. We started by setting them up with notebooks they could use like diaries. During our family times we took portions of Scripture and studied them together, discovering the excitement of meeting with the Lord. We encouraged the children to write down their feelings and insights and anything new they were learning. Then we shared with one another how the Lord had spoken to us through His Word. As the children shared, we assessed their understanding of Scripture and the thought processes which brought them to their conclusions. This was also an excellent opportunity to encourage them.

As the children grew, so did the depth of our studies. We investigated different systems and techniques of Bible study. One of our basic formats was to:

(1) list chapters by topic;
(2) select key verses;
(3) list principles to draw from;
(4) give examples from our own lives of how these principles could be or were being used.

The children really grew in their confidence and enjoyed feeling that they too would "not need to be ashamed, handling accurately the Word of truth."[2]

Working together as a family gave us another extra edge. Not only were we learning together, but we were teaching each other. It was great fun to see Tanya and Todd come up with insights Paul and I had never considered. I've never forgotten Tanya's insight into the book of Ruth. She was impressed by Naomi's care for her daughter-in-law, while I had always looked at it the other way around.[3] Together our family experienced the things God wanted to say. God used Jeremiah 32:8 to tell us to buy our first house when we moved from Illinois to Texas. The children saw how to use Scripture in making a decision.

We also felt it was important for Todd and Tanya to learn how to use basic Bible tools to augment their studies. During our family times we taught them how to use dictionaries, Bible dictionaries, concordances, cross-references, maps, topical Bibles and various translations of the Bible, meshing them all together into a practical study. In addition to expository studies, we showed them how to take a topic and explore it biblically. We also showed them other devotional guides and workbooks but cautioned them in the dangers of letting these replace a personal study of the Bible. There is no substitute for the joy of discovering for oneself an intimate relationship with the LORD.

We used several books in helping the children get started. When they were eight we introduced them to the *Personal Bible Study Notebook,* which has a section called "Five Minutes in the Word." Later they used the *Ten Basic Steps* by Campus Crusade for Christ. There are many other study guides on the market covering almost any subject they might want to explore. Again, however, we would caution you against allowing your children to become dependent on guides. They need to know how to dig for themselves.

Is experiencing a consistent "quiet time" with the LORD

From the basis of knowing the "how-to's" of studying the Bible, we felt the children needed to develop a lifestyle of meeting with the Lord. A "quiet-time" is spent alone with the Lord for the purpose of fellowshipping with Him. It contains the same elements as any relationship: listening, talking, confessing failures, sharing successes, praising, thanking, making plans, sharing events of the days past, present or future — the list goes on. It is not simply a time of Bible study or prayer, although both may be parts of a quiet time. But most of all, a quiet time gives a sense of having been with God and having acknowledged Him as our foremost relationship of the day and an intimate part of our lives.

Paul and I started by sharing our personal quiet times with Tanya and Todd. We felt they needed to see the Lord as our first priority. They also needed to see how we went about our time with the Lord and to catch our enthusiasm about being with Him. I do have to admit we were not always perfect role models; many times we failed, but even when we did, we admitted these failures and told the children how we dealt with them. This was all part of the modeling process. We needed to communicate to them our need for the Lord, and our loneliness for Him and our loss of perspective when we did not take the time to be with Him.

We have some other practical suggestions for helping your child develop a quiet time. First, help him or her find a quiet place to be alone undistracted with the Lord. Second, make sure the child has a Bible he or she can easily read and understand. There are several children's editions, such as *The Children's Living Bible* and *The Children's New*

International Version. Third, provide a notebook and pencil for recording quite-time thoughts. Our children started with a simple "date/thought" format and later worked into outlines and prayer lists. Fourth, help the child choose the best time for having a quiet time. If possible, encourage meeting with the Lord in the morning before beginning the day; but if your child is a chronic sleepyhead, another time may be better. Children need to understand that having a quiet time is a priority and therefore should have priority time. No matter where they go in life or what they do, they will have to handle first things first. Our walk with the Lord is one of those non-negotiables.

The other day I ran across one of Tanya's notebooks she used when she was about eight, and I can't resist including some of her entries.

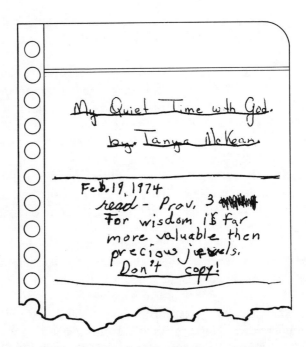

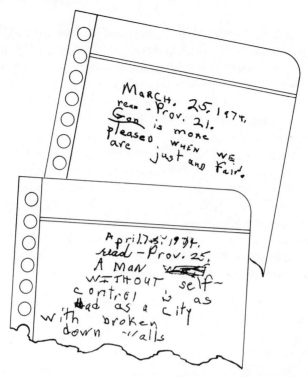

As you can see, in the beginning the children's insights were quite simple. We encouraged them to spend five minutes reading a couple of verses and writing down any observations or applications they made. We often shared those insights during our family time and encouraged one another in our relationship with the Lord.

As Tanya and Todd grew, they deepened in their commitment and desire to be with the Lord. They began sharing their quiet times with others and encouraging them to meet with the Lord. Just yesterday I heard Todd telling a friend she needed to spend more time with the Lord in order to see victory in her relationship with her coach. Our children learned to add elements of worship and praise and found ways to "spark it up" when their quiet times seemed stale. Like any relationship, our time with the Lord is in danger of becoming routine and monotonous. Fathers, think back to your dating days. If you had taken your date to the same drug store every day for the same kind of soda, you probably wouldn't have impressed her very much. But instead you were very creative in finding ways to please her. We need that same perspective in our times with the Lord, creating enjoyable times of worship with Him.

As they grow, children need to develop their own convictions on having a quiet time. Obviously you cannot stand over them the rest of their lives. By helping them experience the presence of God and develop habit patterns of meeting with Him, you will also help them realize the importance of their relationship with the Lord so that they "miss Him" when they haven't been "with Him." Our encouragement throughout adult life is also a key. Just as friends candidly have asked me, "How are you doing with the Lord?" I can love my children enough to remind them gently of their priorities and to encourage them to follow them.

Has a general working knowledge of Scripture

As the children learned from their Bible study and quiet times, they began to catch the picture of what an amazing book the Bible is in its format as well as its content. Its organization and depth of material are incredible. That is why Paul exhorts us to "handle accurately the Word of Truth,"[4] and why 1 Peter 3:15 encourages us to be able to give an answer to anyone who is seeking the truth.[5] The two must go hand in hand if we are to be mature and independent before the Lord.

We began by learning, with the children, the books of the Bible and where they are found. From there we worked on a basic knowledge of what each book is about and the general theme of the book. Later we learned the major divisions of Scripture (i.e., Pentateuch, history, poetry, etc.), when they were written, and their chronological order, historical background and authorship. The "Walk Through the Bible" program is an excellent tool for experiencing the Bible through drama to get an overall perspective.[6] I highly recommend it as a family activity.

As we studied, we also considered some of the themes which hold the Bible together. For example, the demonstration of God's love flows through creation, to the lives of

Abraham and Joseph and through the kingdoms and captivity, on to the love of Christ resulting in changed lives and God's promises to future generations as found in the book of The Revelation. There are themes of peace, joy, obedience, God's character, salvation, deliverance, forgiveness, judgment and many more throughout Scripture. Looking at them broadly forms a solid base that later will stand up against teaching which may seem to contradict what the Bible as a whole has to say on a subject.

Is developing as a person of faith

Every believer experiences times of being faced with difficulties and no solutions. I think of poor Moses standing out in the pasture being told he was going to free the slaves of the most powerful nation of the world.[7] At such times the Christian realizes solutions come only from the Lord and not from one's own resources. We wanted our children to be able to go to the Lord when things went wrong or when they didn't understand what He was doing in their lives. A friend once stated, "Children can only develop their own faith when they are taken seriously and given the freedom to depend on God in their circumstances."[8]

We saw what seemed to be three parts in developing as a person of faith. First, one needs to know how to seek the Lord and trust His faithfulness. Second, one needs to internalize God's promises through memorization. Only when we know what the Lord says can we claim it. And third, one needs to realize that seeking the Lord and memorizing His Word are worthless unless fleshed out through obedience. All three parts are essential to the life of faith.

As in most spiritual education, Paul and I realized the kindergarten of faith was held at home. Our children needed to see us seeking the Lord, memorizing His Word and obediently trusting Him through our actions. As a family we took on things that seemed impossible. One time during the height of the gasoline shortage we traveled to some of our ministry locations in a gas-guzzling Winnebago that slurped up a gallon every eight miles. Needless to say, we were on the edge of faith. As we traveled, we used Scripture to remind ourselves and the Lord that we were His servants and had no provision apart from Him. While crossing New York we became desperate for fuel; every gas station we saw was dry and had been for some time. Together we sought the Lord. Miraculously, in a remote area, we found a station where the tanker had just arrived. Situations like these showed Tanya and Todd God's faithfulness as they joined with us in believing He would do the impossible.

When Tanya wanted to go overseas with a language program, none of us had any idea where the money would come from. Although this was a hard area for her to believe God in, she sought the Lord and felt He really wanted her to go. At first the money seemed to pour in, but toward the end she was still short of her goal. She came to us and asked, "Mom, Dad, pray for me. I only have two days left and the money still isn't here. I don't know where it's coming from, but I do know the Lord has never let us down. He won't let me down now." The Lord honored her faith and every penny came in. She had a tremendous time on the project, but the lesson she learned before she left has been the most enduring. Despite the struggle involved, she had learned to seek the Lord, claim His promises and be obedient to His will.

In order to claim God's promises, we have to *know* God's promises and at any appropriate time must be able to bring them to our minds. That's why we felt it was important that our children "treasure in their hearts" God's Word.[9] We initiated a memorization program using passages rather than individual verses so they would know whole thoughts instead of little bits here and there. Some of the Scriptures they learned were: 1 Corinthians 12:4-8, James 1:2-6 (Phillips Translation), 1 John 5:11-15, Isaiah 41:8-12, Joshua 1:7,8. Other passages are listed in Chapter 13. We wanted to be careful not to give the children the idea that verses are pat answers to problems or clubs we use on God to make Him do our will. Instead, the Bible is an expression of God's heart to the people He loves. We wanted Tanya and Todd to develop God's perspective on different issues. The mentality of "a verse a day keeps the doctor away" can often lead to rebellion and bitterness. God will not be forced into any human's will. However, our faith in Him is reinforced through a knowledge of His Word.

I'm sorry to say that there are no instant formulas for teaching children to seek the Lord; it must be done by example and encouragement. As a family you have to take steps of faith which are beyond your "comfort zone," giving the spiritual response of seeking the Lord room to grow. It's hard to communicate how exciting it was to see our children grow in their faith in the Lord over and beyond their own means.

Has a strong concept of who God is

In order to trust God, children must know who God is. We would be fools to trust our lives to someone who was a liar, cheat and merciless tyrant, yet for centuries men have done just that in following pagan idols. God desired His people to experience Himself in the fullness of who He is, and thus He revealed Himself through His creation, His Word and His Son.[10] As we get to know Him, we can trust Him.

We began teaching our children who God is by using His Word. We taught them the attributes of God's character with a passage demonstrating each attribute. For example, God's loving-kindness is demonstrated in Jeremiah 9:24. By hearing each attribute and then connecting it with an illustration, the children formed a mental picture of what God was like. We also related God's attributes to practical illustrations from everyday life by asking questions such as, "When was someone loving to you?" or "How do you feel when someone is concerned about you?" We reviewed the attributes often until they became a subconscious part of the children's concept of God. We also had them read *Knowledge of the Holy* by A. W. Tozer to reinforce and expand their concept of God. Since this book is a little more difficult than some we had used, we discussed it chapter by chapter during our family times. To this day Tanya and Todd still refer to things they learned through it.

We also taught the children about the character of God through nature. We all love to hike and camp, and we always have spent as much time as we could outdoors. Our love for the outdoors was even part of our consideration in moving up to the mountains. Tanya and Todd still love to stop along the side of the road to watch the sun send its last glow through the peaks onto the clouds below. The squirrels and birds that drive our dog crazy all reflect the balance and justice of nature. It's hard for me to understand why so many naturalists are evolutionists. Even now that Tanya is a college student, when she feels pressured and overwhelmed, she rides her bike or goes jogging to bring back a sense of God's balance through nature.

But Paul and I knew it was not enough for our children to know God's attributes or see them in nature; they also needed to experience them in their own lives. So we encouraged them in their own relationships with God to feel His presence, reflect on His loving-kindness, and experience His miraculous power within their lives. We also encouraged others to share with Todd and Tanya how they experienced God. Tanya really was strengthened in her own walk when her friend Mike shared how God proved His faithfulness by providing the money Mike needed. Such experiences showed God was not a vague force of yesteryear, but a dynamic personality at work in lives today.

Thankfulness is the natural response to realizing who God is. When we understand who He is and see His ultimate power, knowledge and love, we can relax when life doesn't go as anticipated. God would never work toward anything but our best.[11] This is one of the most difficult concepts to teach children (and adults as well), but it is absolutely necessary in the life of faith. We don't like what we don't see; but even though we don't understand exactly what God is doing or why He is doing it, we need to trust in who He is as we allow Him to control our lives.[12]

Again, example is the foremost way to teach children, and I have to admit Paul and I have both stumbled in this area. I remember once when Paul was trying to fix a clogged drain and all the gunk and water came spouting into his face. His disgust and anger were obvious, but not so obvious as they were moments later when Todd innocently reminded his dad to "thank God" for the situation. Paul came pretty near to spreading the glop all over Todd! But later Paul did go to Todd to ask forgiveness and to let him know he was completely right. The Lord was using the drain to teach Paul to give thanks in everything;[13] and although he did not like God's method, he was grateful for the instruction. Together Paul and Todd grew in experiencing who God is.

Has a strong understanding of who he is in Christ

A parent can hardly pick up a book on child-rearing today without finding a great number of its pages devoted to self-image. Christians and non-Christians alike agree that self-image is the one most determining factor in a person's life. If a child has been fed negative comments about himself, he probably will believe them and perform accordingly. But a child who has been reinforced positively probably will have a better jump on life.

But where does the spiritual fit into self-image? Isn't self-image a psychological issue? Just as the spiritual influences every other area of our lives, it also influences our emotions. Jesus did not die just to save us from eternal damnation spiritually, but also to provide "peace," "comfort," "joy," "power," and "abundant life."[14] When God promised to meet all our needs, He didn't say, ". . . except for the emotional ones."

Many of us are scarred by the unkind comments of parents, classmates, teachers, pastors, dating partners and others too numerous to mention. Unless we have some standard by which to measure such comments, we fall prey to believing each and every one of them. God through His Word offers us a standard we can cling to, based on His own character.

I'm not going to cover all of God's provision for a healthy self-image through His Word, since many other writers have done that so well. But I do want to stress the importance of giving children the best possible base for positive self-image. That includes meeting their emotional needs to the best of our ability, giving them knowledge from the Word to fill in the holes left by our humanity, and reinforcing through daily living who they are in God's eyes.

I suggest that you as a parent make sure you have a firm grasp on your own biblical perspective of self-image and who your child is before the Lord. If you suffer from a low self-image, you will probably treat your child in like manner. This is not to say that unless you are totally psychologically healthy you cannot have positive input in your child's life, but it is to say that you should have enough self-awareness to know where you stand and enough vulnerability to communicate honestly with your child when you fail. Recognizing children as "gifts from God"[15] is difficult today in a world which treats abortion so lightly and sometimes seems to see children as inconveniences. Having a firm hold ourselves on the value of the individual is the first step in raising children with a good self-concept.

We need to be careful how we communicate with our children. In our hearts we parents can believe ours are the brightest children around; but if we only point out the "red marks" on the school papers, our children will feel like failures no matter how good the grades are. We must also guard our communication *about* our children. When children hear us talking about them to other people, they may fear we are either spreading the word on their faults or singing their praises so loudly they can never live up to them.

Besides our own influence, Paul and I exposed our children to other influences that would reinforce positive self-image. Quite honestly, any person who was negative and hostile didn't spend much time around our children. I wanted Tanya and Todd to be around people who valued them as individuals. We also encouraged the children to listen to stories and tapes that built self-awareness and God-awareness. Josh

McDowell has a very fine tape called "Self-Image"; and he has recently written a book, *His Image . . . My Image,* which is an excellent presentation of how we are viewed by God. I have listed other suggested books in Chapter 13, but the list is far from complete. It seems as if almost daily I run across something else I wish I had had when the children were younger.

I have a teacher friend who begins every day with a list of the children in her class, then checks off each name after she has found some way to affirm that child. Every child receives some kind of encouragement every day. I can't help thinking that if we as parents made it our goal to encourage our children daily to become who God has created them to be, our world would be vastly different.

Consistently growing in the ministry of the Holy Spirit

I praise God that Jesus did not leave us alone but sent the "Comforter" to be with us.[16] The ministry of the Holy Spirit within our lives provides us with the power and insight to do God's will. Without His ministry of faith, "it is impossible to please God."[17]

In the last few years, with all the controversy around the ministry of the Holy Spirit, some people are so afraid of wrong teaching that they avoid the subject. But in de-emphasizing the Holy Spirit, we rob our children of the knowledge of the power in which to live the Christian life. The apostle Paul encourages us to "walk by the Spirit and you will not carry out the desire of the flesh."[18] Without the Spirit of God, whom we receive the moment we allow Christ to come into our lives, all we can do is carry out the "desires of the flesh."[19]

Paul and I needed to teach our children how to "walk in the Spirit." Children need to know how to "breathe spiritually," to exhale impurity through confession and inhale the fresh power of the Holy Spirit.[20] Like all of us, our children

need to know how to let Christ control their lives and produce the love, joy, peace, etc., known as the "fruit of the
Spirit."[21]

Walking in the Spirit cannot be forced upon anyone. The
Christian walk, like salvation, is a matter of the will. We
cannot make our children walk with God, but we can
demonstrate to them the benefits of such a lifestyle and
give them the instruction and tools they need to make it
readily available.

Paul and I have talked at length with the children about
our walks with the Lord. This is another time when vulnerability is a key. As Todd and Tanya have seen us confess
our sins to the Lord and to others, they have been more
open to confessing their own. I'm sure if they had seen us
with spiritual pride, they would be more apt to struggle
with their own spiritual pride. But through our patient
modeling and encouragement, our children have been quite
open about their struggles. Together we have sought the
Lord and have seen Him win real victory in their lives.

Is committed to prayer

Prayer is simply talking to God, and we wanted our
children to be as comfortable talking to Him as they were
talking to us. We realized that much of what is taught about
prayer is not true communication, but rote memory. I'll
never forget the time our three-year-old Todd bowed his
head to lead the family in prayer over dinner and mumbled,
"Now I lay me down to sleep. . . ." He wasn't half as
embarrassed as I was. I knew then and there we needed to
work on our communication skills.

First we worked with the children on the importance of
prayer. Just as human communication typifies relationships,
our communication with God typifies our relationship with
Him. If we are cold or impersonal, it probably means we're
not experiencing the relationship God intended. If we're
always praying for others rather than our personal needs,
we may be avoiding something. Looking at a person's prayer
life can give a good indication of where that person is in
relationship with God.

We wanted our children to know, too, that God has an open-door policy. He never sleeps, and He never locks the door because He is too busy. In fact, He longs to "give us the desires of our hearts."[22] His resources are vast and His power limitless. We would be fools not to take advantage of such a friend and all He offers us.

We also showed the children what the Bible says about prayer and their relationship with God.[23] We looked at Jesus' prayer life and His relationship with the Father.[24] We had Tanya and Todd learn passages like 1 John 5:14,15 and Matthew 7:7-11. Jeremiah 33:3 was also special to them — "Call unto Me, and I will answer you, and I will tell you great and mighty things, which you do not know."

We set up a prayer notebook for each child. In the beginning we used simple steno pads but lately several good prayer notebooks have come out on the market. At times the children used the prayer notebooks in connection with quiet-time notebooks. The principle was to have them record each prayer request and the date they prayed for it. Another column had space for the answers from the Lord and the dates they were received. We wanted the children to be aware of what they were asking for, to ask specifically, and to rejoice with the Lord over answered prayer. We also knew the prayer notebooks would serve as a record of God's faithfulness.

We were excited as we watched the children grow in their relationships with God and heard this growth reflected in their prayers. When we were looking for a house to buy in Texas, Todd prayed for one with a "park in back." I believed in praying for the impossible, but I hated to see him disappointed. Instead, tears filled my eyes when we found a house with — you guessed it — "a park in back." God does hear the prayers of a five-year-old.

Each person determines the destiny of his or her life. Someone may become a great poet or author or statesman or even preacher, but without spiritual development that person is like a "noisy gong or a clanging cymbal."[25] "Without faith it is impossible to please Him."[26] We wanted

children whose lives reflected their faith in the Lord, children
who were firmly grounded and growing in their love for Him.

Thought questions

Why is it difficult for you to develop your child spiritually?

How should you develop personally in order to foster
your child's spiritual development?

How will a strong concept of God affect your child's life?

6

Physical Development

I will give thanks to Thee
for I am fearfully and wonderfully made;
Wonderful are Thy works,
And my soul knows it very well.

Psalm 139:14

The physical is an area which seems so obvious it's often overlooked. After all, everyone has a body in one form or another, and it usually functions reasonably well. We usually take bodies for granted until something happens to make them not quite so reliable.

But bodies are never reliable for teenagers. Their bodies are in constant change. Their legs grow too long for their pants. Their faces sprout pimples. They never know what they will face when they wake up in the morning. There may be a little stubble or no stubble at all, either of which can be embarrassing. And for a girl, there is the fear of forever being flat chested or, worse yet, of having the boy sitting next to her notice she isn't.

One of the best things we can do for our growing children is to recognize that this area which we take so much for

67

granted is a whole new ball game for them. Each change brings mixed feelings and new responsibilities. To make matters worse, Madison Avenue arrives with a myriad of products and an impossible image for the teens to live up to.

Growing up always has been difficult. Can you remember back to pony tails and saddle oxfords? Or maybe you relate more to the twist and protest signs? A friend told me the other day that as a teenager she had a paper dress. Do you remember those? Now we deal with gelle and mousse and leather skirts with chains. And yet life really is not much different from our own teen years. The stakes are higher because young people have more personal power than ever before, but the issues are basically the same. Young people are exploring the world around them, their bodies and their individuality. Wise parents come alongside to encourage and support them as they develop.

The God who created us knew we wouldn't have an easy road. I couldn't help smiling while writing this, wondering if God created Adam as an adult just to avoid taking him through the teenage years! More seriously, we see the first murder as a result of two young men trying to learn how to handle their bodies and emotions. Blood runs hot during the teen years. On the other hand, this is a very impressionable age for those who have been brought up in the fear of the Lord. Samuel was able to resist following in the footsteps of Eli's sons; David had the naive strength to face not only Saul, but Goliath as well.

God isn't surprised by our struggle to grow. He gave us His Word to help us through our struggles. As in other areas of life, we need to come in out of the world and take on God's perspective. The physical is one of our main battlegrounds with Satan. John reminds us, "For all that is in the world, the lust of the flesh and the lust of the eyes and the boastful pride of life, is not from the Father but is from the world. And the world is passing away, and also its lusts; but the one who does the will of God abides forever."[1]

We wanted our children to have a biblical perspective. God has given us wonderful bodies. Even He stood back after the act of creation and saw it was "very good."[2] Our bodies are something we can be proud of, and yet with the pride comes an awesome responsibility: God wants us to use our bodies to give Him glory each day of our lives. That's a lot to expect from a teen, but it is a part of growing up. Either we will spend life indulging our own desires, or we will spend our lives a "living sacrifice unto the Lord."[3]

The following elements are ones Paul and I thought our children should grasp as they entered adult life. Some may seem very basic, while others are philosophic. But each one builds to the hope and expectancy that with knowledge and physical ability will come strength and power to be used for good and not evil.

Accepts himself physically as a gift from God

So much is made of physical beauty in our society that life is rather difficult for those of us who are slightly less than perfect. Yet beauty is something we see valued from the beginning of history. Genesis records the story of poor Sarah, who was given away three times by her cowardly husband because of her beauty.[4] Helen of Troy nearly lost her nation. Caesar's masculine image eventually led his country to ruin. Since the idea of contests first arose, men have been striving to show off their physical strength; muscles were a sign of masculinity long before the word "macho" was invented.

But the Lord has always cared for more than just our bodies. He cares for the total person. He was not busy somewhere else when we were created; He knew exactly what He was doing. Children love to pick on other children different from themselves, taunting, "He must have broken the mold after He made you." But it's not funny to the victim. He hurts. The sad part is, the children doing the teasing hurt too because they see their own imperfections and are scared to death someone will notice them.

That is why children must understand that God was in control when they were made. Psalm 139 says, "For Thou didst form my inward parts: Thou didst weave me in my mother's womb. . . . My frame was not hidden from Thee, when I was made in secret, and skillfully wrought in the depths of the earth."[5] Not only was our creation wonderful, but the psalmist says a few lines later, "When I awake, I am still with Thee."[6] God did not abandon us to see if we could survive. The Lord told Jeremiah, "Before I formed you in the womb I knew you, and before you were born, I consecrated you."[7]

God is very much aware of what goes on in the creation process. I'm sure understanding this is difficult for parents of children with severe physical deformities. These parents must sometimes feel as if God were absent when the formation process was taking place. I do not pretend to have the answers in dealing with these situations. But I strongly feel we need to confirm to these special children that although they might not have all the looks and abilities they would like, God was involved in their creation and cares very much about all areas of their lives. They still have a responsibility to give what they have back to God in holy living. Their bodies, which may seem useless and ugly to them, are very precious in the Lord's eyes.[8]

The child who doesn't see the physical body as a gift from God will probably become rebellious. It's as if this child is saying, "You blew it, God. Now I'm going to have to take over!" The teenager may try to compensate with an overabundance of makeup or some extreme style of dress or possibly a messy, careless attitude that says, "God, you didn't care so why should I?"

But these rantings and ravings are about as silly as a lump of clay saying to the potter, "What are you doing?"[9] It's obvious what God is doing. No good potter enjoys making ugly vessels! Just look around you and you can see God intends to create beauty. Sin is bent on destroying that beauty through disease or selfishness or, in the case of our children, through judgment and teasing. Our children need a strong base to stand on, one which will give them power to resist all temptations to believe things other than what the Lord has said.

Helping Todd and Tanya gain and keep healthy physical

attitudes has not been an easy job, and Paul and I still have to work at it from time to time. It's hard for teens not to compare themselves — often unfavorably — with others of their age group. But through the ups and downs of daily living we have tried to reinforce the reality of Scripture by reminding the children of the character of God — that He is all-knowing, all-powerful, all-loving, etc., — and by assuring them of our own acceptance of how God made them. Several excellent books dealing with self-image are listed in the appendix, but one of our favorites is *His Image . . . My Image* by Josh McDowell. In it he says

> It is important to realize that we should not make the development of a healthy self-esteem our supreme priority. In reality, a positive self-image is a by-product of pursuing the goal of knowing Christ and of being conformed in His image. Having a healthy self-esteem is not our ultimate goal. Knowing Christ in all His fullness is.[10]

Understands and practices personal hygiene

This section may seem so basic it may be almost embarrassing; but, again, remember that being adults and taking on adult responsibilities is a new experience for our children. We often assume that they have picked up on things just because we do them regularly. Sometimes, however, children are not motivated to copy us or do not see the purposes of what we do. They simply may be waiting for us to tell them they are now mature enough to start. We saw our goal as helping the children understand the reasons for and importance of personal hygiene as well as giving them techniques and tools.

By definition hygiene is a "system of principles for the preservation of health and prevention of disease."[11] More simply, it is the care of the body. The main issue is cleanliness. Individuals usually have their own standards of cleanliness, which vary from family to family, culture to culture. What seems important to one person may seem ridiculous to another. It's important for you as a parent to analyze what you subconsciously do to care for your body and to communicate those practices to your children.

We all know that the curse of the teenage years is blemishes, which can ruin a teen's self-image. Therefore teens should know what causes blemishes, how to wash their faces, how diet affects their oil production, and what medical help is available. But most of all, teens need to accept blemishes as a fact of life. Everybody gets them at some point in life. I recently talked to a teenage girl who was just thrilled to find a pimple on a poster of Ricky Schroeder's face. For the first time she realized she was not the "odd man out" and that a teenager could have a pimple and still be a television star. It's not what's on the outside that counts, but what's on the inside.

Both bathing and dental care, while not so visible as skin care, are important to growing teens. With increased activities such as dance and sports, teenagers need to adjust their habits. They also need to begin using good deodorants. Commercials somehow connect toothpaste to sexual attractiveness, but we encouraged our children to go the extra mile and develop good habits of flossing and rinsing.

Hair can be controversial as a child is growing up. Teens feel a tension between wanting to be like all their friends and wanting to be uniquely themselves. Mix this with a basic laziness and desire to take shortcuts, and you have their favorite hairstyle. We parents need to give room for creative expression while reinforcing basic principles of cleanliness and neatness. We need to help our children see which products are helpful and necessary for their texture of hair and which ones are fancy advertisements. Tanya and I consulted a hairdresser who recommended cuts which would be best for Tanya in light of the shape of her face, the texture of her hair, and the current styles.

Sometimes working with a boy on personal hygiene is more difficult than working with a girl. Girls seem to be more intrinsically motivated by how they look and dress than guys, who like to just "hang around" acting cool. But boys, too, need to realize that for personal safety as well as social contact, personal hygiene is a necessity. Eventually no one wants to be around a stinky, smelly person even if he considers himself a "jock." Even though we don't have to live to please the world, we still don't want to prejudice others against us because of our personal appearance.

Maintains proper weight for his age

I have always struggled with my weight, and I hate the battle; so I wanted to do whatever I could to help my children avoid the same frustrations. First, from the doctor's chart we discovered the ideal weight for each child based on age, height and build. Then we talked about good nutrition and what is necessary in order to lose or gain weight. I tried to set a good example for them in the meals and snacks I prepared. Paul and I also encouraged the children to exercise. We especially had to keep an eye on Todd, since he had a build similar to mine. We have really been pleased with the progress and self-discipline he has shown.

Keeps a regular physical fitness program

A regular exercise program is good not only for weight control, but for improving strength and endurance and increasing potential in other areas of life. Our family chose running as our exercise. Almost daily one or another of us was out there hitting the trail. Sometimes we ran together, but often one of us went alone, enjoying the solitary time with the Lord. Since Tanya has been away at school, she has purchased weights and works out in her room. The means of exercise is not as important as the doing of it — the discipline of mind and body, and the experience of control over what God has given us. It is important to be as physically fit as possible in order to give the Lord the best we have.

Maintains a good diet

"What goes in must come out"; very simply, if you put "junk food" in, then "junk" will come out. Very early, Paul and I wanted our children to understand good nutrition. Like most American families, our biggest battle was with sugar. We tried to set an example at home of making wise nutritional decisions, of learning how to choose from different food groups and of varying menus to avoid eating just a few kinds of food. We also talked about the dangers of cholesterol, and we watched our fat intake.

Some families have children who are sugar-sensitive. My friend's daughter gets terrible headaches when she has too much sugar. This mother handles the problem by stressing natural consequences: When the child gets a headache, her mother gently reminds her where the headaches come from and what she can do to avoid them. Since the headaches are uncomfortable, the little girl has learned to regulate her own sugar intake. This approach does not work on nutritional situations where the result is removed from the offense, but it does build a sense of responsibility and makes a direct connection between how we feel and what we have eaten.

Has at least one sport he is confident in

Being good at a sport or some kind of physical activity not only builds our bodies but develops us emotionally. Few people will deny that these factors are related to maximum health. When our children reached the age of ten, we encouraged them to take up any sport they wanted to try in order to see what they enjoyed. Tanya went out for soccer, track and bicycling; Todd enjoyed soccer and baseball. Eventually they narrowed their interests, but in the meantime they were exposed to several different sports and could feel confident trying new kinds of physical activities.

Sports also encourage teamwork and relationships. Through sports our children found friends with common interests. Todd and Tanya competed against each other, encouraging each other to give the best performance possible. This was exciting for me as their mother because I no longer had to say, "Go out and get some exercise." Instead they were excited about seeing if they could get good enough to whip the "Spartans" or any other team threatening their ratings. They also saw the importance of good nutrition, discipline and exercise modeled by coaches and teammates.

Has regular medical checkups

Just like car maintenance, caring for the body is not a

"do-it-yourself" job but often needs the assistance of experts. We may add oil to our car and feed it gasoline, but from time to time someone needs to look under the hood. Neither Paul nor I came from a family which stressed medical maintenance, but we felt our children needed to know what outside sources of information are available. We made it a priority in our schedule to have physicals once a year, dental visits twice a year and eye exams every two years.

We also encouraged our children to see a doctor if a situation warrants it. I know many families where the mood is, "We don't want to bother the doctor with a little thing like this," when the child really feels he is hurting. I'm not suggesting we rush to the emergency room with every skinned knee, but often a child grows up ignoring symptoms which need attention just because he is afraid to get professional help.

We also wanted our children to know that some physical problems require the help of specialists. Quite honestly, Todd and Tanya's teeth were a mess, and eventually this started to affect their whole self-image. They were afraid to smile for fear someone would notice their crooked teeth. A trip to the orthodontist confirmed what we already knew. Even though the correction was costly, we knew it was important to the children's health and self-image. The same was true about glasses and eventually contacts. Part of the excitement of these times came from the way we saw God provide the money for these expenses. It confirmed that God cares enough to meet all our needs.

Maintains a good appearance

As we said before, appearance is not everything, but it often gives the first impression others have of us. Therefore it is important that our appearance reflect what is inside us. Every person is unique and created as a special gift from God. Expressing ourselves through our looks is part of the fun of being a person. It's as if each one of us is an artist working with the color and form God has given us. Our "works of art" are what others see when they look at us.

Tanya and I had a great time learning together in this area. First we got some expert advice from several beauticians on what would be best for our hair. We did the same with makeup, clothes and "colors." We really enjoyed talking about what we liked and didn't like, and thus we avoided the battles of "Mother wants this, daughter wants that." We neutralized potential conflicts by following the advice of professionals. Of course, we could (and sometimes did) go against their advice, but we did so as a matter of educated choice. Taking Tanya to experts made her feel important and showed her I thought it was worth the effort to have her know what others had to say. I have a friend who is an avid teen-magazine buff just so she can keep up with her daughter's latest fashions.

We also tried to include Tanya's friends in much of what we did. I remember when we had a cosmetics party in our home. Tanya, then in ninth grade, invited some of her classmates and friends. We had a great time eating popcorn and learning about different skin types and how to work with them. Subtly it showed the girls that what may be good for one person is not necessarily good for another. It also built the girls' self-esteem as they heard about their uniqueness and how to make the most of themselves. We did the same thing with a beautician who concluded with some comments on the "inner beauty" attainable through a personal relationship with God. Not only was it a good learning time for Tanya, but it was great exposure to the gospel for her friends.

Boys don't seem to be as concerned as girls about appearance, but don't let them fool you. Just try to get a boy to wear an outdated haircut and watch his reaction! Rather than emphasizing attractiveness, talk with your son about "appropriate" looks or "fitting in" with others. Right now it is important to him to "fit in" with his group, but he needs to be aware that there are certain standards of appearance he needs in order to impress a coach, get a job or win the girl of his dreams. Isn't it funny how a guy sharpens up when he wants an attractive girl? Boys know how important appearance is, even if they would never admit it. I remember when a girl suggested Todd part his hair on the left rather than the right. It's never been on the right since.

Dressing appropriately is important for both guys and girls. Nothing is more awkward than being inappropriately dressed. Children need to know what "appropriate" means in our society and how the meaning differs in various parts of the country. Here in California, "anything goes;" but our children could be embarrassed to visit their friends in New York if they aren't aware of what the standard is on the east coast. We wanted our children to feel confident around others, free to be themselves and enjoy others without their physical appearance standing in the way.

Real beauty is on the inside of a person rather than the outside. 1 Peter 3:4 tells us it's "the hidden person of the heart," not the "braiding of the hair, and wearing gold jewelry, or putting on dresses," which is attractive to God and others. The outside should simply be a reflection of what the Lord has put inside. If the outside is a mess, other people will not be attracted to us or curious about the "hidden person" inside. 1 Timothy 2:9 tells us our adornment is not our outward appearance but "the living of a good life." We wanted children adorned by their lifestyles.

Has a biblical perspective on sex

Why do most parents break into a cold sweat when talking about sex? I admit it's a lot easier to talk about soap and water than parts of a male or female body. Most of us parents received inadequate sexual training; and because we obviously have filled in the blanks enough to have children of our own, we may be tempted to feel that our children will do the same. And they will. But what they'll miss in such an approach is perspective. Their friends on the street will not have the maturity or experience we parents have in communicating sexual information, and they probably will miss the Christian perspective. Even if your education and communication skills are weak, remember they are much better than those of a fourteen-year-old who only knows bad language and porno pictures. From whom would you rather have your child learn?

Paul and I wanted our children to have a biblical perspective on sex. God looked down on the human body and saw it was "good;"[12] so He commanded Adam and Eve to "be fruitful and multiply."[13] He also commanded them to leave others and "cleave" to each other.[14] They enjoyed such intimacy that even though they were naked, they were not ashamed.[15]

We wanted children who would not be ashamed of sex, but would be free to enjoy all God has given them in this life. We also wanted children who respected God's gift of sexuality and determined personally to use it for the glory of God rather than for selfish gain. Sex, like anything else in this world, can be used for good or for evil.

I don't want to go into a detailed explanation of the biblical perspective of sex except to say it is beautiful. Often parents struggle in their presentation of sex because they themselves do not understand or experience what the Lord has to offer in this area. In working through this area with your child, realize how your experience may cloud what the Lord has to say. Also be sensitive to what the Lord would want to teach you personally. You may have made mistakes, but refreshment through forgiveness can bring new freedom.

Believing "attitudes are caught and not taught," the first thing we did in communicating sexual attitudes to our children was to reflect consistently a respect and enjoyment of the human body. We were careful not to use trite names for sexual organs but to call them what they are; we never joked about them but treated them as respectfully as if we were talking about ears or eyes. We let the children know that no subject was off limits, but that some were best approached in private conversations.

When the children were about ten, we started them on a reading program. They started out with *Almost Twelve* by Kenneth Taylor. Then as a family we read Dobson's *Preparing for Adolescence* and discussed it chapter by chapter. This helped us evaluate Tanya and Todd's comprehension and to compensate for their age differences. When they were fourteen they read *The Stork is Dead* by Charlie Shedd. As we look back we feel the greatest value was in the communication opened by the discussion of the books, sometimes father with son, mother with daughter or as a whole family.

But, realizing sex education is not a textbook situation, we tried to be sensitive to our children's lives and to help them apply what they had learned through books and discussions. I can remember when Todd came to Paul about some locker room talk he'd been hearing. Even though it was difficult, Todd told the guys, "Hey, look! If you want a girl who's pure for yourself, then why not keep yourself pure for the girl you want to marry?" Tanya took a stand in her psychology class during a debate on pre-marital sex and homosexuality. She and two other girls presented the alternative of a godly lifestyle and encouraged the class to examine their personal convictions. It took courage for both Todd and Tanya to do what they did, but it built character. To encourage them in their convictions, Paul and I met with them several times a year to see how they were doing and to reinforce God's perspective. We also assured them their feelings and desires were not abnormal but part of God's plan.

As the children grew and became more deeply involved in relationships, we tried to keep communication open and to reinforce truth. We emphasized positive outlook rather than condescending attitudes. Now that Tanya has already gained her independence, we are not in a position to determine what she does or doesn't do; but we can remind her of the benefits of waiting until after marriage to enjoy sexual relationships, and we can counsel her on ways to avoid excessive temptation. We have also talked about what has happened emotionally and spiritually to those who didn't wait.

More than anything, we wanted children who had personal convictions concerning relationships. As they got older, magazines and books like "Campus Life" and *Preparing for Adolescence* encouraged biblical perspectives by giving strong intellectual and practical information on the Christian stand. Counseling with mature Christians like youth leaders and summer counselors gave Tanya and Todd balanced perspectives in dealing with their emotions. Through many influences they are becoming stronger in the conclusion that sex God's way is the best way.

Even though we no longer live in a world of pony tails and butch wax, some things remain the same. Physically, kids struggle with the same struggles we somehow survived. They fear rejection because of their appearance, feel clumsy with their new growth and are uncertain of the future. Our job as parents is to assure them of who they are and offer them the confidence to spread their wings and fly.

Thought questions

Why is self-acceptance so important?

How do you reinforce a biblical perspective of beauty to your child?

How can a biblical perspective on sex affect a child's future?

7

Intellectual Development

"He who knows not and knows not he knows not is a fool; show him.

He who knows not and knows he knows not is simple; teach him.

He who knows and knows not he knows is asleep; wake him.

He who knows and knows he knows is wise; follow him."

Arabic Apotheam, Manner 4

Just as a person cannot function without a body, his contribution to life is limited by his intellectual development. Traditionally, the three parts of an individual are body, mind and spirit. In the intellect the realities of the world and their functionings mesh with the spiritual truths which govern them. Unfortunately, humans tend to glorify what has been created rather than the Creator, patting themselves on the backs for discovering what God already knew, and teaching their children to do likewise.[1] The challenge of the intellectual development of children by Christian parents lies in teaching them to be "in the world but not of the world."[2]

Besides humanism, Christian parents face another challenge in dealing with intellectual development — social pressure. The two areas in which children are most likely to be evaluated by others are the physical and the intellectual. Grandparents gloating over their grandchildren often say, "Isn't she a beautiful baby" or "I can't believe he can smile already!" The child's toddling steps and first words are recorded in a baby book, emphasizing from the very beginning that being pretty, smart and coordinated is what is noteworthy.

The situation doesn't improve as time goes on. Have you ever thought about the bases for granting college scholarships? Men get them for physical adeptness, displayed through sports; women compete in beauty pageants. For the young person who is neither a bruiser nor a beauty, the alternative is to excel intellectually. I have yet to see a scholarship given to a social butterfly for her social skills or to the below-average student for his emotional development in handling failure.

Christian parents face the constant challenge of intellectual balance. We want our children to be exposed to the world and its knowledge, but we also want them to realize a person is far more than what he knows. He is also what he feels, believes, enjoys and does. Parents must be careful not to allow the child's self-image to become entangled with grades, but to encourage development in all the areas, each area supporting the others. I remember a time when Tanya was struggling with her math; she just couldn't seem to master it. The harder she tried, the more she felt like a failure. At the same time she was excelling in track. We simply showed her how the different areas of life balance one another. That gave her the space and positive attitude she needed to tackle the math problems and eventually conquer them. She was beginning to understand that our goal is to glorify God as He has created us, freeing our minds, bodies and spirits to develop to their full potential.

Has working knowledge of basic academic skills

The first intellectual element we wanted to look at was the children's working knowledge of academic skills. We strongly believe in the importance of reading, writing and arithmetic. Without understanding in these areas, a child is often needlessly handicapped for life. We needed to know our children's proficiency and to provide special help if needed. More and more we hear of students who somehow get to college without reading beyond a fourth-grade level. I don't mean to suggest everybody has to make straight "A's"; but we as parents should be able to tell if our children are grasping academic concepts and developing in their reasoning ability. We need to keep track of their homework, their progress in school, and their performance in class.

Although much has been said for and against Christian schools, we decided to send our children to public schools. As a result, we were more aware of what they were studying than most other parents we knew. Our children were exposed to an everyday laboratory of the world's thoughts, which we helped them compare with God's thoughts. They had firsthand experience with being "salt" and "light" to others. Todd was ecstatic when, because of his witness, he was asked to lead his soccer team in prayer. Of course, every parent needs to decide which school setting is best for each child; but we felt our involvement with the public schools increased our awareness of the children's learning processes and our understanding of the direction of education in our country.

Has read twenty world's classics

Along with their basic reading skills, Paul and I wanted each of our children to read twenty books from a "world's classics" list for junior-high and high-school students, obtained from our local library. Such a reading program may sound unusual at first, but we felt it was beneficial to expand the children's background in literature to which they otherwise might not be exposed. I can remember my own embarrassment when someone referred to a book, assuming

I was familiar with it, when I didn't have any idea what
they were talking about. We also felt such reading would
expand Tanya and Todd's vocabularies and writing styles.
And we saw the historical value of classics as they reflect
the styles and world feelings of various time periods.

But most important, classics reflect people in real-life
situations and show the importance of how they handled
those situations. Whether their solutions were good or bad
determined the outcome of their lives and, in many cases,
the outcome of the world around them. That is what makes
these stories "classics." We felt our children needed that
broad perspective in their lives. We gave them full freedom
in their choice of books from the list and encouraged them
as they checked off books read. We tried to pace them at
four a year, but they enjoyed the first year's reading so
much they surpassed their quota.

Has a general grasp on world history and current events

A study of history teaches much about life and living.
Through the centuries people have tried every imaginable
type of living style, with varying results. A general knowledge
of these experiments and their consequences prepares us not
only for personal choices but for societal choices.

Paul and I both enjoy history and have done quite a bit
of traveling. We have taken the children with us when
possible, helping them to see history not just as events that
happened a long time ago, but as factors that have made
a particular country or part of a country what it is today.
The concept of heritage makes people uniquely who they
are. We also have used books and travel films from the
library to communicate what has happened in the world.
Periodicals like *National Geographic* give an intergrading
base to history past and history present. We have taken
Tanya and Todd to the library to pick out historical novels
and biographies at their own levels so they could feel the
human side of history.

But the most benefit has come from talking through the impact of world events, past, present and future. As we traveled we tried to relate what we saw to what the children had learned in their studies. When Tanya was fourteen we stopped at Williamsburg while traveling through Virginia on business. We let Tanya teach us what she knew, and then we learned together the impact that little village had on history. Sitting in a room in the Capitol, we could almost feel our ancestors laboring over the wording of the Bill of Rights. Times like these bring history to life!

Paul and I discussed current national and world affairs with the children. We live in a fast-paced world, and in order to make intelligent decisions one must grasp what is going on. That means we as parents must take the time to keep ourselves informed. We talked to the children about political issues, helping them understand the history behind the issues and the impact they will have on the future. We prayed during terrorist attacks in Iran and around the world, and tried to help the children see not only the ugliness of the situation but the desperation of the people. We often talked about the sin of the world and how it leads to tragic events.

Believe it or not, history can be fun if we seize opportunities and make the most of them. Traveling cross-country can open conversations in history for weeks to come. Even small children can enjoy pretending what it would be like to live in the White House or to be a settler. It's fun to think about the feelings, hardships and joys people had in those unique situations.

And if you can't travel, television can come to you, opening a world of information. I've been amazed at the social issues covered in prime-time television. "Call to Glory," which reviewed the social issues of the 1950s, had a powerful impact on a friend's child as she felt for the first time the injustice of prejudice. Even situation comedies cover issues from pre-marital sex to alcoholism. Sometimes the opinions expressed do not reflect a "Christian" standpoint, but usually they present two sides of an issue and work through it in an almost-true-to-life manner. Of course, news broadcasts, educational television and network specials also broaden perspectives. One added benefit in this television-oriented world is that when children realize history is good enough to make television, they feel it must be important.

But even with all the exposure available through media, I am still amazed at how uninformed in current events some people remain. One person asked me the other day if Chairman Mao was still alive! I feel it's a tragedy that many Americans refuse to vote because they don't know the issues. If they don't know the issues, it's because they haven't taken the time to investigate them. As a result, they put the power of the government into the hands of few. I don't want Tanya and Todd to be embarrassed by not knowing what is going on in the world. Instead, I'd like to see them encouraging others to learn from the past mistakes of history, making a better world for themselves and others.

Knows how to find needed information

Obviously, a person cannot know everything about everything, but he can look like he does if he knows how to obtain the information. We must realize that the world God has created does not begin and end with our own knowledge but is broader than any one mind. As we cooperate and put our knowledge together, we grow personally and as a whole.

The library became our second home when our children were little. Not only have Tanya and Todd grown familiar with the exciting fiction section, but we have shown them how to use the card catalog and reference sections. We have shown them the various dictionaries and encyclopedias and thesauruses which can help in expanding their vocabularies. We also have shown them how to gather more recent information from periodicals. Some libraries even have listening rooms with record libraries.

We also felt the children should have a good grasp on the thought process involved in doing research as well as the mechanics of finding information. They need to realize that although they may feel ignorant about a subject, they have access to more information.

Knows how machines work

Today's society is based on mechanics. Machines wake us, heat us, cool us and then lull us back to sleep. Paul and I felt our children needed some basic information in how machines work, especially in the areas of physics and chemistry. Although they might never need the expertise to create or repair machines, they did need to know the principles of basic maintenance. In other words, they needed to know enough to decide whether a leaky sink needed a plumber or could be fixed easily using some basic knowledge.

One machine I would like to mention at this point is the computer, something which did not even cross our minds seven years ago. I can't believe how it has affected our lives in these few short years. Looking ahead, it seems it will be extremely difficult to exist in our world without a working knowledge of computers. Again, it isn't necessary for the children to know all the fine points of programming, but they should understand basic programs and the principles behind them.

Knows how to drive

The other machine which has taken over our lives is the automobile. Instead of being a privilege, as in past generations, automobile ownership is viewed today as an American right. The other day I heard some seventh graders talking about the kinds of cars they expected when they got their licenses. Some of the talk was dreams, but much of the expectation was real; and the dreams of some of those children will come true.

The responsibilities of driving are probably among the first adult responsibilities children will have. They need their parents' help in accepting these responsibilities and handling them maturely. We had our children take driver's education in school to establish their basic knowledge and skills and to give us a break on insurance. The school was equipped with films, practice rooms and simulators which were much safer than the ol' brown Plymouth!

Since car responsibilities do not end with road skills, we also had the opportunity to teach finances, maintenance and moral responsibility. Both children were responsible for their own gas money, insurance payments and basic maintenance of the cars. It was just as important for Tanya to know when and how to add oil as for Todd. If she was going to drive, she needed to know how to take care of her vehicle. Both children also needed to know the seriousness of their privilege. Believing in the sanctity of life and the reality of death has done a lot to help them both mature.

Has a practical knowledge of general skills

General skills may or may not get anyone a job, but they are necessary for successful daily living. Paul and I felt both Tanya and Todd needed basic cooking, washing, ironing, sewing and household repair skills, as well as the ability to care for their tools. We have worked on these skills with both children, boy and girl, so that when they move away to college or into the working world, they will know how to take care of themselves.

Tanya, who has been at college this past year, has been flabbergasted by the number of students at school who don't know how to wash their clothes, clean their rooms, coordinate outfits or sew buttons on. She has seen their embarrassment and fear of new situations. These poor kids may be whizzes in geography, but they feel like failures in the little things of life.

Recently Paul went out to help one of the girls who works for us, when her car broke down, and in the process he asked her when she had some maintenance done. She looked at him as if he were speaking a foreign language; so he tried to be more specific. "When did you last get your oil changed?" She didn't seem to know so he asked, "When did you check it last?"

She looked puzzled and said, "Check the oil? How do you do that?"

When Paul tried to show her how, he found the hood of the car was rusted shut. Through all the years this girl had owned her car, she had never before done one thing for its maintenance. She thought all she had to do was drive it.

Men are not immune to practical ignorance. One young man who worked for us followed me into the kitchen and asked if he could "just watch." To break the awkwardness of having an audience while picking a chicken, I asked this college graduate about himself. As the story unfolded, I realized this young man had never done anything for himself. The only thing he could cook was hot dogs. He also didn't know how to do his laundry. He was humiliated by his ignorance in these everyday tasks and was embarrassed to mention them to anyone. Instead he let his inadequacies eat away at his self-confidence.

These illustrations do not stand alone. We've seen many college graduates academically prepared for success but personally headed for disaster. I have heard of Christians who have ruined their testimonies because of the filth in their homes — to the point where others refuse to eat on the premises. We wanted children who personally felt successful and available to witness for the Lord.

In taking care of ourselves and our belongings, we need to remember that all we have comes from the Lord.[3] We are responsible for wise use of all we own; we call this the principle of stewardship. Stewardship relates to everything we possess — time, talents and material goods. Knowing how to fix something is useless if you can't find your tools or if you don't set aside enough time in your schedule to do the work. Stewardship involves being responsible to the Lord for all He has given us.

We have added a few more skills to the list as time has gone on. We wanted both the children to know how to put a balanced meal together and how to shop. I know it took me awhile to figure out how to buy a ripe cantaloupe and what kind of lettuce was best; I wanted to save my kids from eating sour fruit. Tanya and Todd needed to know how to make wise use of their money at the grocery store. We have also worked with decorating skills, teaching the children how to make comfortable, warm surroundings and set a mood. A home is a reflection of its owners, and Todd and Tanya have learned how to create an atmosphere they and others can enjoy.

Is developing creatively

When God talks about making man in His own image, it is interesting to note that He does so in the context of creation.[4] I can think of few things more satisfying to anyone than to create something and then take a step back and be able to say, "This is good."

Creativity is really a thought process — the ability to look at a situation and develop a plan for working it out. Mixed with learned skills, the plan becomes reality. Often creativity is confused with artistic ability.[5] Creativity may be expressed artistically, but it may also be conceptual and practical.

Paul and I wanted our children to know the joy of creation. Tanya did not really enjoy needle crafts, but she became competent enough to know she could do them when she wanted to. What she did enjoy was creating beautiful photo albums. Todd worked more in the areas of carpentry and electrical design. I can remember his first go-cart. It looked more like a collapsed wagon; but he was proud of it, especially after Paul gave him a few suggestions for its improvement. Todd really likes fixing things, using his creative abilities to solve problems.

Creativity can even be expressed in such mundane activities as planning a meal or painting a wall. Projects need not be executed perfectly or be prize winners to be satisfying. Creative times are great because of their freedom of expression, call to excellence and care of details they offer.

Knows intellectually the "whys" of his belief

Although it may sound as if we are repeating some of what we said about spiritual development, we felt it was important that our children have an intellectual base for their faith — a base that could stand up to any debate. Too often Christianity is viewed as an emotional experience without an intellectual foundation; this is simply not a true picture.

Through study and research it becomes very obvious that no other faith is more soundly based than Christianity. One of the children's first assignments was to read Paul Little's book *Know Why You Believe.* Together we discussed the book and learned how to handle challenges to our beliefs. We also exposed the children to top lecturers and pastors who were strong in applying what they believed rather than giving pat answers and lists of rules. We also showed Todd and Tanya how to get more information about Christianity, how to judge the information for validity, and how to present it to others. Josh McDowell's books, *Evidence That Demands A Verdict,* Volumes I and II, are excellent.

Our children's ability to defend their faith was important for two reasons. First, we didn't want them to become confused or influenced by others who might sound more knowledgeable than they. Instead, we wanted them to know without a doubt that their faith was not only experiential, but practical. Second, if we are to be a light to the world, we must be able to shine.[6] Peter encourages us to be able "to give an account for the hope that is in you."[7] People around us need to know the truth about the salvation our Lord offers. We wanted Tanya and Todd to be able to express their faith not by becoming defensive, but by offering information and encouraging others to make decisions.

Is teachable

The teachable person is open-minded to new ideas and thought processes. I love the Chinese proverb, "Mind like umbrella. If not open, doesn't work" A closed-minded person soon begins to die intellectually. We never wanted our children to feel they had a corner on truth, for fear they would be filled with the haughtiness and pride God despises. At the same time, we wanted our children to be able to discern what knowledge coincides with Scripture or has intellectual validity. Much of the information which floats around and is presented as truth is really only speculation. Children need to know which information to accept openly and which to reject.

The issue of teachability is really an issue of selfishness. Unteachable people reject knowledge because it wasn't their original idea and because new ideas may threaten principles they have built their lives upon. When we are open to the thoughts and information of others, we can experience richness, freedom, and flexibility in our lives. Paul and I wanted children who were eager to learn about everything around them, but who also had wisdom to discern when they were being deceived.

Knows and uses principles of management

Along with intellectual knowledge, we felt our children needed an understanding of basic management principles. We live in a fast-paced world where time and organization count, and those who do not manage time and effort wisely fall behind. We especially felt the children needed to learn to escape the tyranny of the urgent — to pace and organize their projects. They needed to know how to work effectively as well as to create "down time" for relaxation. They needed to develop good study and work habits as forerunners to the discipline needed later in their chosen career fields.

Small efforts in this area have had huge payoffs. Just buying the children their own alarm clocks helped them to schedule their time independently. We showed them our filing system and encouraged them to keep track of their own personal papers. There are many creative ideas for helping your child develop management skills. I have one friend who has bought her daughter a timer to help her set goals in doing her homework.

Has a sense of ethics

Knowledge abused is a terrible thing. One can use identical skills to save lives and to commit murder. We have seen this over and over again through history as countries and leaders have used their expertise to annihilate their enemies. Paul and I wanted our children not only to have knowledge, but to have a code of ethics — a standard of conduct and moral judgment — to which knowledge could be applied.

We wanted a part of the children's code to be based on the simple question, "What would Jesus do in this situation?" Together we have read the book *In His Steps* and have talked about current issues in light of the life Jesus lived. Since both Tanya and Todd have received Christ, they desire their lives to be a reflection of His. 1 John 2:6 says, "He that says he abides in Him ought himself to walk even as He walks."

Another line of questioning we taught the children to use was, "Is it true? Is it kind? Is it necessary?" Whenever we were tempted to use our knowledge to cut people down rather than build them up, we just reminded ourselves of this little series of questions. Proverbs 17:27 also reminded us, "He who restrains his words has knowledge," while 16:24 encouraged, "Pleasant words are as a honeycomb, sweet to the soul and healing to the bones." This doesn't mean we should skimp on the truth; we are told to "speak the truth in love."[8] This does not always come naturally. In fact, it is usually an act of our wills, but it is an act that pays off in the lives of other people.

The main issue is, "Does it honor the Lord?" Much of the knowledge available to us would not honor God but would glorify man's warped sense of right and wrong. 1 Samuel 2:30 promises, "They that honor Me, I will honor." We do not honor the Lord when we use our knowledge to cause weaker Christians to stumble.[9] In spite of all our knowledge, we have to come back to the verse, "Whatever is not of faith is sin."[10] Knowledge can be used for good or evil.

We all need wisdom in using our knowledge. Wisdom is the practical application of all that we know. But even if we have the knowledge of geniuses and the wisdom of sages, without the spiritual dimension, our lives are like fading grass.[11] We wanted our children to understand that knowledge is important, wisdom is precious, but the Lord is life itself.

Thought questions

How does your child feel about school?

Where do you see your child as being "gifted"?

How does a person develop a sense of personal ethics?

What can he or she do to uphold personal ethics in spite of the actions of others?

8

Social Development

"It is with the awe and the circumspection proper to them,
that we should conduct all our dealings with one another,
all friendships, all loves, all play, all politics.
There are no ordinary people.
You have never talked to a mere mortal."

C. S. Lewis[1]

According to *Webster's Dictionary,* society is a "community of related, interdependent individuals."[2] Whenever two people relate with each other, they establish a form of society. Very simply stated, society is relationships.

But how we handle those relationships is our choice — and not an easy choice. Our own lives are so complicated that it's sometimes difficult to deal with others at the same time. Yet, when we don't have relationships, we suffer from a sense of aloneness.

Adam felt those feelings of aloneness, and in all of creation that aloneness was the only thing God saw as "not good."[3] So He created Eve as a "helper suitable for him" (Adam) to relate to. God has also given us relationships so we won't suffer from aloneness; but, sadly enough, what occurs in our relationships often is disastrous. Sin takes what God made available and uses it to cause pain. Eve used her relationship to persuade Adam to sin.[4] Relating to others carries a great responsibility because it affects not just us, but also those around us.

Each one of us is a unique creation of God and therefore worth getting to know. As C. S. Lewis said, "There are no ordinary people." Can you imagine a world in which people realized they were touching something immortal as they touched the lives of those around them?

We wanted children who were motivated by the LORD in their relationships. We wanted them to feel confident in social situations and make others comfortable too. We wanted them to act responsibly in the decisions made by society. But most of all, we wanted them to reflect the LORD as they related to others.

Understands the biblical motivation for relationships

I'll never quite understand why God chose to use humanity to spread His message of salvation. Instead of revealing Himself in some dynamic, cosmic manner, He chose to come to the earth as a human. Through relating with others, Jesus demonstrated the character of God to the point where people were willing to believe what seemed impossible — that Jesus Christ was God incarnate. Then Jesus left this world, giving the disciples the responsibility of conveying to others, by their lives, words and actions, the character and truth of His words. After experiencing human frailty, I cannot imagine why God chose this method, but He did. Through our relationships we have the opportunity to reflect Christ to others.

The world has its own perspective on relationships and that perspective is basically self-centered. The world advocates that we have relationships for what we can get out of them, that we use people to make us feel good, affirm who we are, and help us reach the goals we desire.

But what if the world's system doesn't work? What if people don't make us feel good? Instead, what if they ridicule us or criticize us or actively try to keep us from attaining our goals? It is critical that our young people have a biblical perspective on relationships and a clear knowledge of why they relate to others. Certainly we do have our needs for warmth, affection, encouragement and stimulation met by others, but the basis for our relationships lies in the provision of God Himself.

As one becomes more secure in his relationship with God, he is freed in his relationships with others. We wanted our children first to be secure in their relationship with the Lord, then to be secure in their relationships within the family. Ross Campbell explains,

> The home is stronger than any other influence in determining how happy, secure and stable a teenager is; how he relates to adults, peers, or children; how confident he is in himself, and how he responds to new or strange situations. Regardless of the many distractions in the life of a teenager, the home has the deepest influence on his life."[5]

Third, we wanted our children to develop in their relationships with their peers. Interaction with people their own age was an important step in handling rejection and peer pressure. And fourth, we wanted children who could feel comfortable in any group of people solely because of who they knew they were.

Luke 2:52 tells us, "Jesus kept increasing in wisdom and stature, and in favor with God and men." The apostle Paul said, "I know how to get along with humble means, and I also know how to live in prosperity."[6] He also said, "I have become all things to all men that I may by all means save some."[7] Both Jesus and Paul had the ability to find favor with others and yet to stand for truth in the face of opposition. Scripture shows us how men of God were sensitive to local customs and showed respect for the people they related to. At the same time they were in no way weak or wishy-washy but were men of integrity. We encouraged our children daily to get along with others and to enjoy relationships as God intended, yet to stand firm in the things they knew were true. I love the way the apostle Paul expressed it in Romans 12:8, "If possible, so far as it depends on you, be at peace with all men."

Has taken responsibility, as a part of society, for its actions

Just as an individual must take responsibility for personal actions, a group of individuals must also accept responsibility for its corporate actions.[8] This is true not only in government, but in every group to which we attach ourselves. If we belong to a church, we are responsible for the doctrinal stand of the church, its reputation, its finances, the discipline of its members and the consequences of any decisions the church makes. When a young person hangs out on a street corner with a gang, he assumes responsibility for the actions of that gang; if the gang is caught stealing, although he may not touch the stolen goods, he is a part of their decision to commit the act.

I am amazed at how few children understand this simple principle. Somehow they feel that if they stand in the background, watching some childish prank but not initiating it, they will be absolved of all responsibility. But when I see that these children's role-models are adults who know of violent crimes but are afraid to "get involved," or who gripe about "government rip-offs" but don't bother to vote, I know why the children feel as they do. The products are passive, apathetic children who grow into passive, apathetic adults and form a passive, apathetic government. This often results in a few activists taking control while the rest look on in a daze, mumbling, "What has happened to our world?"

We felt it was important for our children to recognize their responsibility for the groups they were involved in, no matter how insignificant the groups might seem. We encouraged them to be active in Sunday school classes, school projects, clubs and sports. We also encouraged them to express their opinions within the groups and, if a group was violating their integrity in some way, to have the strength to leave the group and do what they personally felt was right.

This was not easy for Todd and Tanya, especially in peer relationships. I remember when, as much as he hated it, Todd had to drop out of a community boys' club because the sponsor was vulgar and demeaning toward the boys. It was hard to leave his friends and the club's outings, but the Lord gave Todd peace about his decision. A few weeks later he joined a little league team with a Christian coach who did a lot to encourage him as an individual. It took courage for him to walk away from his club, and I was proud of him for taking responsibility and choosing his group associations wisely.

Paul and I encouraged the children to be aware of and actively involved in political issues. I have a friend who takes her children into the voting booth with her to demonstrate the process and privilege of voting. At our house we discuss various referenda. I know of others who have taken their children into city hearings, visited state legislative bodies, and let their children write to congressmen and newspapers regarding issues about which they felt strongly. Children need to feel they are a part of their nation, to grow in their responsibilities as citizens to the point of taking part in the decision-making process.

Is confident in the role of host, hostess or guest

Part of relating to others is knowing how to create an atmosphere which will meet a need in another person's life. Usually we think of "entertaining" in a formal sense, but whether we are aware of it or not, we do a certain amount of entertaining in almost every social contact. A sensitive host or hostess subconsciously has a purpose for inviting someone over. He or she tries to create an atmosphere where the guests' needs — emotional, financial, physical, or whatever — can best be met.

For example, if a young mother I know needs to get out of the house and identify with others who are going through similar struggles, I probably wouldn't invite her to a lecture on "Terrorism in Politics." Instead I might invite her to a Bible study, with child care available, where she can meet with other young mothers experiencing the same frustrations.

If I know a young missionary who is looking for financial support, I might arrange a formal dinner party for friends who would be in position to help him. In both situations I assess the need and think how I can meet it.

Children need to learn similar skills. Tanya once gave a surprise party for a friend who was feeling exceptionally lonely. Another time, when one of her friends was struggling with family problems and needed someone to talk to, Tanya invited her to spend the night; and in the wee hours of the morning, the girl's pain overflowed.

Entertaining also meets the needs of companionship, fun, enjoyment, recreation, physical exertion and intellectual stimulation. Todd told me the other day he enjoys Scott because "he makes me think." There are many reasons for social settings, and we need to understand how to structure situations to best meet needs.

Let me add that it is perfectly acceptable to structure social situations to meet your own needs. I have a friend who celebrated her thirtieth birthday by giving her friends each a rose and telling them all how much they meant to her. Needless to say, she avoided the depression which hits so many at that age. When neighbors greeted another friend with a cold-shoulder treatment, she took the initiative and invited them to her home for a Christmas dessert. One of the neighbors later commented, "She just didn't know we don't do things like this out here, but I'm sure glad she did it." She did it to meet her own need for relationships, but in the process she met the needs of others.

Paul and I also wanted our children to feel comfortable as guests. They needed the social skills to be able to respond to invitations graciously and, if unable to attend, to communicate their appreciation for the invitations. They also needed to know how to respond to their host, to help if it is appropriate, to be served or honored by others, and to communicate appreciation afterwards either verbally or by note.

Todd and Tanya also needed to know what is "socially acceptable" in various circles. Singing "The Ol' Gray Mare" might be fun around a campfire but inappropriate at a retirement dinner. They also needed to be confident in the use of eating utensils and table manners. We role-played formal dinners at home with a full array of silverware, crystal and china. We knew habits like elbows on the table and slurping soup had to be dealt with at home before they spread to other places.

When Paul and I were first married, we were sponsors of a youth group. We had all the kids registered for camp when one boy told us he couldn't go. After asking a few questions, we discovered he had decided not to go after he found out we planned to stop at a restaurant on the way. He was fifteen years old and had never eaten in a restaurant. I prayed that day, "Oh, Lord, help me to train my children to meet any circumstance. Don't let them live in fear."

Knows common etiquette and courtesies

Opening a door for a woman or seating her at the table is fast becoming a lost art in this day of "women's rights." But what most people don't realize is that they are stripping away an honor, not an insult. Scripture encourages us over and over to honor others — mothers and fathers, fellow believers, husbands and wives, employers and rulers. Peter sums it up by saying, "Honor all men; love the brotherhood, fear God, honor the king."[9]

When Paul opens the door for me, it isn't because he thinks I am incapable of doing it for myself. My goodness, any woman who has carried as many laundry baskets and suitcases as I have can certainly open a door for herself! But instead he wants to honor me, to tell me in this little way I am special to him. I honor him by receiving his gift of courtesy graciously. In turn, I may open a door for a woman at the grocery store. Courtesy is not necessarily a sexist expression, but a consideration of others.

We wanted our children to know and practice common courtesies. Since etiquette varies in different parts of the country, I hesitate to give a list of courtesies. Instead, I encourage you to sit down and make your own list of the things you feel your children should know and practice.

How can they honor others — male, female, elders and children? What is considered appropriate in formal settings? How is your section of the country different from other sections? I knew one woman from Houston whose family had very formal dinners served at 8:30 P.M. Needless to say, she suffered a real shock when she found herself in "farm country" where supper was at five.

I also want to add some thoughts on dating etiquette. Let's face it, dating is an awkward situation. At no other time does your child feel so vulnerable. There, sitting in the next seat, is the embodiment of lifelong hopes and dreams, while your child feels clumsy and unprotected. Under pressure like this a young person tends to do one of two things: either try to put on such a perfect performance as to prevent all possibility of rejection; or act as if it's "no big deal." The etiquette of the occasion becomes either too tense and rigid or too "hang-loose." Either way, the young person has robbed his or her date of the honor really due that special person.

As teens begin dating relationships, they need help in social courtesies. Their tendency is to want to look "cool" like "The Fonz" from "Happy Days." But the real world doesn't always appreciate such images. To honor their dates, their dates' parents and friends, young people need to act with a certain amount of respect; and this respect must be developed as a way of life, not as a performance, so it will continue long after the wedding bells have rung. We have talked at length with our children on how to call for a date, how to accept or reject a date graciously yet truthfully, how to accept rejection and listen objectively to the reasons, how to pursue tactfully and when to quit pursuing. We have also talked about and lived through breakups and have learned to handle them with respect. The children have continued to respect former boyfriends and girlfriends for who they are even though the relationships did not endure.

Is confident in making introductions

Getting to know people is often awkward, and the use of social courtesies makes it a little easier. Proper ways of making introductions can be found in any etiquette book. Keep in mind that we make introductions not solely to "follow the rules," but to honor special persons and to establish bases for relationships.

One key to introductions is to find some interests the two persons have in common. For example, Tanya could say, "Mom, I want you to meet my roommate, Carol. Carol, I'd like you to meet my mother. Mom, did you know Carol's parents are missionaries in the Philippines? My mom was in the Philippines last summer." From there the conversations can flow. If you can remember that introductions are the beginnings of relationships, you can keep from reciting formulas and can help meet needs.

Teens, in their desire to be creative, find the wildest ways to answer the phone! You never know if they'll grunt, "Huh?" or quip, "Joe's Bar and Grill." Without putting down their creativity, you must teach them common phone etiquette. This is essential to good communication because phone conversations lack the physical clues which let the participants know whether they understand each other.

We trained our children to receive calls, take messages, make calls, handle wrong numbers, reject obscene phone calls, and renew bad connections. We also taught them how to handle sales and nuisance calls. Just as in face-to-face encounters, telephone users who want to be respected must verbalize respectability.

Is able to relate to various age groups

The cycle of life is amazing and each phase touches our everyday social world. Paul and I wanted our children to have respect for life and for people in each stage in it. We felt it was important that they be as comfortable in a nursing home as in a nursery school. People are people, and as such they have needs in common. The issue again is to discover the needs of other people and try to meet them through your encounter.

I remember the first time Tanya went with her youth group to a nursing home. She was just petrified; she didn't know what she would say to the "old ladies." But by the

time the visit was over, Tanya didn't even want to leave.
Years later, when Grandpa came to stay with us while he
was dying of cancer, Tanya handled the experience with
grace and maturity far beyond her years. She had learned
to value the lives and wisdom of older people, and thus
she was able to minister to Paul's dying father during the
last days of his life.

We can relate to children in the same way. Each little
life holds all the potential of a president or a convict. We
need to discern children's needs and then produce the best
conditions for meeting those needs. How children mature
will depend to a great degree on how adults relate to them.
They have the same feelings as we adults and, in the
simplicity of their youth, great wisdom. No wonder Jesus
taught, "Unless you are converted and become like children,
you shall not enter the kindgom of heaven. Whoever then
humbles himself as this child, he is the greatest in the
kingdom of heaven." Jesus goes on to warn, "And whoever
receives one such child in My name receives Me; but
whoever causes one of these to stumble, it is better for him
that a heavy millstone be hung around his neck, and that
he be drowned in the depth of the sea."[10] Children are
important to the Lord, and the simplicity of their faith can
expand our own worship of the Lord.

Caring for children outside one's own family has a multiple
ministry in the lives of others. First, it gives the parents a
break and time to relate to each other. Second, it gives
children the chance to relate to another individual. I've seen
babysitters have good and bad influences; babysitters will
be perceived as role models and should act accordingly.
Third, it ministers in the life of the sitter. Todd really likes
babysitting because he sees children as "little people with
little hearts and needs." I've seen him grow in his personal
tenderness and giving spirit as he's been caring for chidren.

Puts others at ease because he is at ease

We wanted children who could put others at ease because
of their self-confidence and their ability to handle social
situations. Wherever we have gone, we have tried to include

the children as if they were adults. We never talked down to them with "baby talk," but communicated respectfully with them on their level. Following our example, our friends have done the same. As Tanya and Todd grew older it was not difficult for them to make the transition to adult social settings, because they had been there before and knew what to expect.

God has given us the job of relating to the world. No matter how good our intentions, if we turn people off by our actions, they will never really hear us, see us, or recognize the Christ who lives within us. We will then find ourselves enduring a lonely existence which is simply not necessary. Our desire for ourselves and our children is that we may be all God created us to be — reflections of His love and grace.

Thought questions

Simply stated, what is the biblical motivation for relationships?

How can you model citizenship to your children?

Think through how you can role-play:

(1) being a guest of the governor for dinner;
(2) refusing a date from a boy you can't stand;
(3) introducing a girl to a boy who you hope will ask her out;
(4) your reaction to an old woman you don't know who has just kissed you.

9

Emotional Development

For as he thinketh in his heart, so is he.

Proverbs 23:7

A person is far more than a body or a brain — more than who he knows or what she accomplishes. The essence of a person is what he or she feels. There, in the hidden self, lies the motivation for living and believing. Beneath all the outward trappings, the makeup and high fashion, the degrees and offices, the marriages and acquaintances, lies the true person.

The Bible tells us, "As he thinketh in his heart, so is he."[1] If Hitler's heart had been known from the beginning, I doubt that World War II would have occurred. People put forth tremendous effort to hide their hearts, sometimes motivated by greed, fear or anger. Often it becomes difficult to share ourselves even with our closest relationships; sometimes we even begin to believe our own lies.

Paul and I wanted our children to be free in their emotions. We wanted them to be able to express themselves to others, to receive and to be received by others. Although everyone experiences fear, we wanted our children to be able to process their fears and overcome them in the power of the Holy Spirit. We wanted Todd and Tanya not to deny their emotions, but to use them in their walk with the Lord.

Emotional development is one area in which Paul and I admit we are not experts. We are in the growth process ourselves. We have "hang-ups" and "holes" I am sure we have not yet even discovered. But even in this position, God has given us children to raise and a will to raise them well, and I am sure God knew what He was doing when He did so. We want to share with you some of the ways we wanted to see our children develop emotionally.

Has a sense of significance as a person

We've heard it called every name in the book: self-image, self-concept, wholeness, worth, self-love, significance, identity — every psychologist seems to have another term for it. But all these terms refer to the same idea: our children need to develop a sense of who they are and learn to love and accept that individual. We have already talked about self-image in connection with spiritual, physical and intellectual development; and, at the risk of repeating ourselves, we would like to make a few more comments centering on the emotional.

The denial of emotions is a disease running rampant in our country, becoming somehow tied up with masculinity, women desiring to "become equal," capitalism and Western Christianity. Boys are taught not to cry; women are told they can't do certain kinds of jobs because they are "too emotional"; we don't want our emotions to get in the way of "making money"; and we feel we have to "deny all and take up the cross." Christ never intended for us to deny who He created us to be. Instead He desires that we give ourselves to Him as a "living and holy sacrifice, acceptable to God."[2] But somehow when we think of our emotions, we feel terribly unacceptable to Him.

Self-acceptance involves acceptance of all of ourselves, not just the parts we like. This includes accepting our emotions as well. Genesis tells us we were created in the image of God.[3] Have you ever thought about the emotions of God? If you look at Scripture keying in on the emotions of God, you will be amazed to find that God experiences anger, jealousy, frustration, disappointment, joy and sorrow, as well as many other emotions.

Then why are we so ashamed of our emotions? One of the many reasons is that emotions make us extremely vulnerable. After Adam sinned, he experienced guilt, and his reaction was to hide his "nakedness."[4] When we expose ourselves emotionally, we feel naked. What we don't realize is that we don't have to hide. God walked in the garden many times with Adam when he was naked.[5] God saw all of Adam. But when Adam became aware of good and evil, he also became aware of his own sin and the ensuing feeling of guilt.

That brings us to a second reason to hide our emotions — our fear of rejection. I am sure Adam was afraid of God's response to his sin. I wonder what God's response would have been if Adam hadn't hidden himself or relied on lame excuses for his sin, but had taken responsibility for his actions and asked forgiveness. When we stand naked in our emotions, we run the risk of rejection. It's a very scary position — so scary, in fact, that some of the bravest men think they must deny their feelings. However, we forget God is not only just but loving. Adam did not die on the spot as he feared, although eventually he did die physically. Through His own son, Jesus Christ, God made a provision for eternal spiritual life and freedom from sin's curse. God does not allow us to stand naked, but clothes us with His healing power.[6]

If we only could hang onto these simple truths in our everyday living! Instead we become fearful of the people around us, of their acceptance or rejection, and allow their feelings toward us to determine our feelings about ourselves. These fears begin in the cradle — a fact which makes our job of parenting crucial to our children's development. As we meet our children's needs, we are letting them know there is a good world out there that accepts their needs. We also model to them a good God who wants to meet their needs. But if children live in fear that their needs won't be met — if they are told to "be quiet and go away" — they will do just that and will take their emotional needs with them.

We have been told that eighty-five percent of the adult personality is formed before a child is six years old.[7] By the time our children hit the teenage years, they are well-grounded in their images of themselves. If not for the grace of God, I would throw up my hands in despair! Instead, I have seen miracles in the lives of adults who have trusted the Lord to heal the scars of childhood.

Self-acceptance has spiritual roots. Scott Peck defines love as "the will to extend one's self for the purpose of nurturing one's own or another's spiritual growth."[8] As we love ourselves, we experience spiritual growth. And, "we love because He first loved us."[9] It is a circular effect.

Paul and I felt the first thing we could do for our children's self-love was to love them unconditionally. Dr. Eugene McDonald tells us, "Unconditional acceptance of an infant is the precursor to healthy self-acceptance which enables him to make the most of himself within the framework of his personal strengths and limitations."[10] To the best of our ability, we met our children's needs. And as they grew, we tried to be careful to protect their developing images of themselves. Like many parents, we were inclined to have "pet" names for the children, but we were always careful to pick ones with positive connotations. I can think of many names we could have called our active, into-everything, never-able-to-stand-still little boy, but Paul chose "Sunshine" for him. He felt it reinforced Todd's radiant joy of living.

Even when the children were babies, we told them of God's love. As they got older, we taught them songs and verses about God's care for them. When the children were old enough to study, we all learned together of God's love and acceptance. We memorized verses which became part of Tanya and Todd's thinking. Since "perfect love casts out fear,"[11] we knew if they were enjoying God's perfect love, they would never have occasion to fear Him.

Has a sense of belonging

Very closely associated with self-image is a sense of belonging. Infants have difficulty realizing they are apart from their mothers. Not until babies are about ten months old does it dawn on them that they are separate beings.[12] A sense of belonging replaces a sense of attachment as a child becomes secure in his new identity as an individual.

We realized being part of a family is very important to a child. In fact, this never ceases to be important even when the child has grown. A certain amount of our identity lies with our family; if in nothing else, we are identified together by name. In order to develop a sense of family, Paul and I worked hard to build memories and establish family traditions. We put Sunday afternoons aside as our family times. The Christmas tree always went up Thanksgiving weekend, complete with the little village Tanya and Todd loved so much. One year we weren't home for Christmas and the children commented the thing they missed the most was the little village. We also created what we called the "McKeans' pile of stones." Inspired by Joshua and the children of Israel,[13] we painted rocks and wrote on them things God has done for us, His provisions for us, our answered prayers, and our personal miracles. We also created picture albums to remind us of our times together. One of Tanya's favorite pastimes when she comes home from college is to drag out the albums and go through them one by one.

Even if we hadn't developed a sense of family with our children, they now belong to a greater family — the family of God. We encouraged Todd and Tanya to get to know their "brothers and sisters" and to include them in their circle of love. On Thanksgiving we invited people who were away from their families to enjoy Thanksgiving with us. The Lord has a lot to say about Christian fellowship, about being part of a body instead of individuals simply floating around.[14] As we sense God's salvation in our lives, we also become aware of being a part of Him.

Is accepting of others

After learning to accept ourselves, the task of learning to love others is relatively easy. Jesus tells us to "love your neighbor as yourself."[15] If we are able to look past our own faults and give ourselves room to grow, it is much easier to look past the faults of others and allow them to grow.

Paul and I felt it was important that our children have the maturity to receive people from other cultures with open minds and hearts. Our children have traveled with us extensively and have been in many difficult situations, but I have been impressed with their ability to accept other people's cultural backgrounds and relate to them on a personal level. Wherever we have gone we have found people with the same basic needs in their lives. This obligates us more than ever to share the gospel sensitively with those who have not had the opportunity to hear.

Of course, the hardest person to accept is that strange guy down the street, and there seems to be one on every block. I remember when Todd and Tanya just couldn't stand one little boy in our neighborhood. He was a cry-baby, a cheat, a liar, and had a loud mouth. But we knew he had no father at home. His mother worked odd hours. In reality the boy was crying out for love. Our family times have been crucial to working through relationships as we have prayed and trusted God together for His perspective and love for others.

Is able to make decisions

The better one knows oneself, the easier it is to make decisions. The decision-making process is always difficult because it involves risk no matter which direction we go. The key is in being able to assess clearly where the least amount of risk lies.

Paul and I have taught our children to use what we call the "sound-mind principle" found in 2 Timothy 1:7 (King James Version): "God has not given us the spirit of fear, but of power, and of love, and of a sound mind." Often decisions are determined by fears rather than by the power of love and reason. We encouraged our children, first of all, to pray for the wisdom and guidance of God. Second, they were to make lists of all the pros and cons for each of their alternatives. Their pros and cons were not just to be intellectual, but also were to reflect their feelings on the alternatives. They were to mark those which had special emotional weight. Usually, through this process, one alternative came out ahead of the others; and at that point, as difficult as it may have been for them, they made their decisions. Then they told the Lord they felt they had chosen wisely but knew He was big enough to close the door if they were not in His will. Then they moved out in faith.

Children need to realize that an emotional sense of loss often follows a decision. We can't have everything we want, and it's difficult to make choices. But we also gain a sense of independence when we know we have determined our destiny for ourselves rather than being pawns in the game of life. When Todd was trying to decide whether or not to participate in his school's "senior prank," it all sounded harmless. But as we thought through his schedule, how he had just spent four days working ten hours each, and how he was emotionally drained from the Thanksgiving festivities, we realized taking part would not be a wise choice. But we also knew he would be the one to have to face the first class of the morning with classmates asking, "Why weren't you there?" We let Todd make his own decision and live with the consequences.

Understands, makes and carries through on commitments

Closely related to decision making is the making of commitments. Americans today are very weak in making commitments. They seem hesitant to back political parties, fight for causes, or even get married. They're afraid of being disappointed, of feeling betrayed when their causes or their champions fail. That's why it's important to think realistically about all aspects of a situation before becoming involved.

Once we have made commitments, however, we need the discipline to stay with them.

This is especially true in relationships. Scott Peck writes, "Genuine love implies commitment and the exercise of wisdom. . . . It is for this reason that commitment is the cornerstone of the psychotherapeutic relationship."[16] As we desire to share our lives with others, we grow in our ability to commit ourselves to them and to their personal growth. It's a give-and-take relationship — we give and we also receive. In giving we *do* receive.[17] We receive the fullness of sharing another's life.

Paul and I wanted our children to be strong in commitment, and from their early days, we encouraged them in this area. Whether a situation involved the soccer team or the church youth group, we encouraged the children to think through the pros and cons, make a decision and stick with it. This is not to say a commitment cannot be broken, but if we find ourselves wanting "out," we should go through the same process of pros and cons that led us to our decision. Have conditions really changed, or have we just lost the initial infatuation of the situation? Commitments should be taken seriously; they give us security and a basis for growth.

Is able to have fun and enjoy life

Life is not just a list of boring commitments, but should also include commitments to ourselves to have fun. Laughter is "an expression of the eyes and countenance indicative of amusement."[18] The Bible tells us, "A cheerful heart does good like medicine but a broken spirit makes one sick."[19] I enjoy looking at the life of Christ and seeing the subtle humor He uses.

Enjoyment is different things to different people. Tanya likes talking with a friend or biking, while Todd prefers soccer or downhill skiing. What is important is that both children are free to enjoy what gives them pleasure rather than being tied up in the expectations of others. As our pastor, Rob Zinn, once said, "Joy is not what we feel, it's what we are."

Is able to communicate his feelings to others

One of the biggest needs in a teen's life is to be heard. As they struggle for equality, they want a vote in the world around them. The problem is often they lack maturity and wisdom in what to say and how to say it. In other words, the things they say sound dumb. I can remember when Tanya once proclaimed, "Let's move to China where there is no peer pressure on what you wear," without realizing the ramifications of what she was suggesting.

A wise parent needs to look past what the child is saying to why he or she is saying it. Conversation often takes place on two levels: the intellectual and the emotional. We usually respond to a person on the intellectual level because this contains less risk, but often arguments arise because the issue is more emotional than intellectual. When Tanya suggested living in China, she was motivated by a fear of not being "in" because of her clothes. It would do no good to explain the impossibilitiy of her suggestions unless we met her fear. Instead, it would make her more fearful not only of being "out of it" but of losing our respect and her identity. Several good books on communication are available, but I recommend *How to Really Love Your Teenager* and *Between Parent and Teenager,* both of which deal with your children on the level of their needs.

We also need to help our children learn that communicating includes both expressing and listening to what others say. Paul and I are both committed to talking through misunderstandings with the children until they are resolved. Often this means restating what we meant to say until it becomes clear. Teens need to understand that often others have unexpressed emotional motives, and it does help to try to see through the words to the feelings. For example, when a parent refuses to give a teen permission to go on a ski trip over Thanksgiving, the teen may assume it's because the parent doesn't trust him or her. However, the decision may be more motivated by the parent's desire for family unity and togetherness. Realizing hidden conversations can make handling the real issues far easier.

As a family, we talk a lot. We use the dinner table as one of our major clearing houses. We also try to spend time with the children each night. It fits well into their pattern of praying at night; it's natural for them to go from talking with us to talking with God. We ask questions (being careful not to pry) and share our own daily joys and frustrations. Some of the questions we commonly use are:

What have you been thinking about lately?

How do you feel about it?

What was the hardest thing you had to handle today?

What did you enjoy about your class (friend, etc.)?

What relationship was stressful for you today? How did you handle it?

We receive our children's responses and identify with their emotions. If they are open to suggestions, we make them; but mainly we want to let them know that what they have to say is important to us.

Is able to give emotionally to others

We live in a self-oriented society. All around us we're hearing, "You deserve a break today," and "Experience the best." But the Lord offers us another way of living — that of sharing ourselves with others. This means more than sharing our monetary wealth, but also sharing our emotional wealth.

The Lord has performed healing in all our lives by giving us eternal salvation and security.[20] One of the things Paul and I have helped our children learn is how to share with others the way to experience a personal relationship with God. *The Four Spiritual Laws* and the *Good News* glove are excellent tools we have taught Tanya and Todd to use in explaining the plan of salvation. We have also taught them how to use Scripture in counseling others. We have stressed to them that the Lord desires to use our arms to reach out to others with His love. People don't just want to hear verses but they also want to see demonstrated in others what God offers.

It's easy to see how important our own emotional health is in reaching out to others. We must be sure of ourselves first, and then give to others from the strength of our position in Christ. I do encourage you to teach your children to be wise in their giving of themselves because at times others may consciously or subconsciously take advantage of them to avoid their own growth. Our children don't want or need to become "mothers" to others. But as God has given good things to us, we should be available to give good things to others. God has given Tanya a very special ability to sense the needs of others and reach out in encouragement and wisdom.

Is able to handle emotionally difficult situations

Let's face it, this is where the rubber meets the road! It's one thing to feel good about ourselves when we're doing well, but it's another thing to feel good about ourselves right after we've experienced failure. When life is darkest, we need to draw on the strength which has been building during easier times.

One thing we have taught our children is to identify their feelings and accept them as a part of life. For instance, after losing a job, it would be natural to feel let down, angry and defensive. Unless those feelings are acknowledged, they will fester into bitterness and depression. But we need to go beyond those natural feelings to other things we know are true. For instance, I might say, "I know I am not a failure and that God must have something else in mind for me. I also know the boss has faults which might have led to my being fired. I need to recognize my own faults and the effect they had on my work." From there we need to move on, wiser and encouraged, assured the LORD has not forsaken us but desires to walk with us as we trust Him.

One of the most difficult situations our family ever faced was the death of Paul's father. Dad came to us after he had been diagnosed as having throat cancer; the doctors estimated he had two months to live. Together our family decided he would spend his remaining days with us.

Watching Grandpa die was one of the hardest things any of us had ever done. But we knew we could handle it in one of two ways. Either we could be bitter, questioning God's will; or we could accept His will and enjoy the little remaining time we had with Grandpa. We chose the latter, making his last five weeks an incredible time of learning, of listening to him reminisce about his childhood, and of sharing his secrets for a consistent walk with God.

Nothing can describe the pain we felt for him as we watched him waste away before our eyes. And nothing can describe the pain we felt as we lost not only a father and grandfather but also one of our dearest friends. But turning his last days into a positive experience of love helped us all get through it. We didn't deny our feelings of sorrow and loss, but worked through them until we could rest in the peace of God's perfect will.

I know the children had their own struggles in losing Grandpa. Tanya was expecially close to him. Two years earlier, when Grandma died, Tanya asked to spend her spring vacation with Grandpa, cleaning and cooking and helping out the best she could. Those were ten special days she will always cherish. From a human perspective, Todd and Tanya had every right to be upset and angry at God for taking someone so precious. But instead they met the occasion with an attitude of thankfulness for the opportunity of having a grandfather so dear. Todd commented at the funeral, "I want to be godly like he was."

During times of trouble we have tried as a family to focus on James 1:2-6. In the Phillips Translation it reads like this:

> When all kinds of trials and temptations crowd into your lives, my brothers, don't resent them as intruders but welcome them as friends. Realize they come to test your faith and produce in you the quality of endurance. So let this process go on, until that endurance is fully developed and you will find that you have become men of mature character with the right sort of independence. And in the process, if any of you meet any particular problem you cannot handle, you have only to ask God who gives liberally and generously without making you feel foolish or guilty."

Grandpa left us a great heritage; but of all the things he left, I think none was greater than the character which was built into us through his death.

Thought questions

How much do emotions control your child? What do you think you can do to influence them either way?

What experiences in your child's past have helped develop a sense of security?

When was the last time your child had trouble getting along with someone? How did he handle it?

10

Financial Development

He who is faithful in a very little thing is faithful also in much.

Luke 16:10

Every society has some form of economic system. It may be as simple as bartering or as complex as Wall Street, but as long as one man has something another man wants, some system of trade exists. Every society also has some form of "pecking order" — the "haves" and the "have nots" created by the financial system. And, within our economic system, our children will have some amount of money to spend, save or invest during their lifetimes.

The challenge of parenting is to teach children wise use of their own personal resources, great or small. We have many resources. Our physical bodies allow us to work and earn money. Our intellects provide us with ideas and information others are willing to pay for. Our emotions encourage us to share our incomes with others and give us feelings of pain or pleasure as we use our money. With God's help we have spiritual power over the obsession with money which can distort one's sense of priorities.

Money, like everything else, can be used for good or evil. Daily we witness divorces related to financial tensions. For centuries wars have been fought and men have been killed because of simple greed. On the other hand, most social work today is possible because of the donations and sacrificial giving of some people for others less fortunate than themselves. Money itself, how much or how little you have, is not the issue. The issue is the emphasis you give to money and the control it has on your life.

We wanted children who were free from the love of money,[1] free to pursue whatever directions the LORD had for them without being bound by the dollar. We also wanted children who were willing to trust God to meet all their needs and who would be faithful with the financial responsibilities the LORD would give them. In this materialistic world, we knew we were going against the grain; so we developed our action points carefully.

Has a biblical perspective of finances

Sometimes we tend to limit God's realm to the spiritual aspects of life and forget His omnipresence in everyday living. However, the Bible has much to say about finances — what we have and don't have, and how we should use what we have.

First, we need to recognize that everything we have comes from God.[2] He gives us the capacity to earn money. "Lady Luck" does not determine if one man prospers while another doesn't; God allows men to prosper for whatever reasons He desires.[3]

Being able to accept God's authority frees a person from feeling unduly responsible for his financial position. This is not meant to be an excuse for poverty, but Jesus did say, "For the poor you have with you always . . . but you do not always have Me."[4] Instead of pursuing riches we are to pursue a relationship with God. In return, the Bible promises, "The blessing of the Lord brings wealth."[5] Sometimes this refers to monetary wealth, but often the blessing of the Lord is a life fruitful in benefits far more satisfying than money. We are released when we trust Him to give blessings as He sees fit.

Recognizing our finances as from the Lord also produces a sense of gratitude. It's easy to be grateful when we receive something from nothing. When we recognize God as the God of the universe and ourselves as mere humans, we can be grateful for the power and influence He does give to us. I love King David's response to greatness as he prayed, "Mayest Thou increase my greatness and turn to comfort me."[6] David knew that greatness in power, finances, intellect or any other area brings a responsibility for which a person needs God's power.

Second, in the Bible God has provided principles for the use of money. There are too many principles for me to go into them in detail, but one example is in Proverbs 27:23,24, where God encourages us to "Know well the condition of your flocks, and pay attention to your herds; for riches are not forever, nor does a crown endure to all generations." God also tells us to "calculate the cost" when beginning a project because "otherwise, when he has laid a foundation and is not able to finish, all who observe it begin to ridicule him saying 'This man began to build and was not able to finish.'"[7] Both of these are principles the world recognizes as sound money management. I would recommend *Giving Yourself Away* and *The Financial Planning Workbook* for further study into biblical principles of finance.

Third, the Bible warns us about the emotional impact of money. Like the "desires of the flesh" in the physical realm, the "desires of the eyes" (the desire to have what we see) in the financial realm can have a powerful impact on our decisions.[8] Jesus warns us in Mark 10:25 that "it is easier for a camel to go through the eye of a needle than for a rich man to enter the kingdom of God." Instead, God encourages us to "seek first His kingdom and His righteousness; and all these things shall be added to you."[9] We need to learn to control our desires while making the most of the resources the Lord has given to us.

Last, there is the spiritual principle of tithing, which is our response in accepting God's authority in our finances.

In Malachi 3:10 we are told to "bring the whole tithe into the storehouse" and God will "open for you the windows of heaven and pour out for you a blessing until there is no more need." He also promises in Proverbs 3:9,10, "Honor the Lord from your wealth, and from the first of all your produce; so your barns will be filled with plenty, and your vats will overflow with new wine." If God is who He says He is, it only makes sense that we honor Him in direct relationship to the way He has blessed us. It is not a matter of owing but of giving back to God in order to enable Him to bless us more.

God cares what we do with what He has given us. When Todd was six we gave him a fishing pole. We cared how he treated it. If he had left it lying around, we would not have been motivated to give him anything else. But when he received it in gratitude, took good care of it and even wanted to share the little fish he caught with it, we were delighted and looked for other ways to give to him. As we are responsible and follow the Lord's guidelines for our finances, we're blessed by the freedom He gives and by the trust relationship we are able to build with Him. There is joy in obedience.

Has a giving heart

In accordance with the biblical perspective, Paul and I wanted our children to experience the joy of giving. After experiencing all that God has given to us, not only monetarily but personally, our response should be a desire to give to Him and to others. There is a difference between tithing and giving: tithing is what the Lord has asked for from our income; giving is what we offer, over and beyond the tithe, as an expression of our affection. Tithing is a matter of willing obedience; giving is a creative expression of care.

We encouraged our children to do one worthwhile selfless giving project each year. One year they provided Christmas presents for a family who didn't have resources for gifts. Another time Tanya and Todd joined with others to provide presents for battered wives and their children. They also have supported missionaries. Tanya gave books from her own library to a cousin living overseas who had read all the books available to her. We helped the children see that giving involves not just money, but also time and caring. Recently a friend's husband died, leaving her with two preschool children. Todd has offered to go over and wrestle and do "man stuff" with the kids. A giving spirit goes far beyond money as an expression of the heart.

Knows how to work

In an interview for *Worldwide Challenge*, Bill Bright stated that the one thing he felt was being overlooked in the raising of children was "the value of work," and I regret I have to agree with him.[10] Instead of a work ethic, children seem to have the goal of seeing what they can get away with in life. Instead of pursuing excellence, they want to see how much they can get for the least amount of effort.

Yet I see people personally dissatisfied with their careers, complaining about having "just a job." Few have personal goals, and those who do, measure them in dollars. Last week I heard an interview with a lawyer who has the goal of earning a million dollars before he turns thirty. I can't help thinking the world might be a better place if his goal were to represent the cause of justice in a sinful society without considering personal gain. He might receive more personal emotional satisfaction from comforting those distressed by the legal system than from struggling with stock market reports. However, it seems success in the world's eyes is defined by the amount of money one possesses.

But success should be measured by the personal satisfaction of knowing one is honoring the Lord with his labor. In some ways, this satisfaction is similar to the joy of giving. Instead of giving money, we provide a service or product for the use of others; and the pride of giving our service or product can be related to the concept of "working unto the Lord."[11]

"The laborer is worth his hire,"[12] and we should be proud of doing our jobs well. We should feel a sense of reward as we receive our paychecks. We work to provide for our families and loved ones, and there is honor in this. 1 Timothy

5:8 says, "But if anyone does not provide for his own, and especially for those of his household, he has denied the faith, and is worse than an unbeliever." Those are pretty strong words! Individuals who work and provide for themselves and others should have a sense of personal satisfaction.

Often we become negative about work and look at it as a necessary evil. Work is a part of God's command to "subdue the earth" and to be "victorious" over it, which is a high calling, not a punishment.[13] We all wish there weren't so many "weeds" around so life would be easier, but that's not the way it is. Our children pick up our attitudes. If we grumble on our way to work, they will grumble as they take out the garbage. If we punish them with extra chores, then they will view work as negative. But if we praise them for jobs well done, show them how much we are enjoying their products and affirm the prices they had to pay to produce them, then they can even overlook the temporary pain of their work.

When we were in the process of moving to our present home in the mountains, Paul was out of the country on moving day; so the children and I tackled the job. But Todd and Tanya went over and beyond the call of duty when I got sick with the flu. They unpacked all the boxes and got the house habitable while I lay helplessly in bed. It cost them a great deal to miss school and lug those boxes up two flights of stairs, but they were willing to pay the price; and Paul and I let them know how much it meant to us.

Understands how to manage finances

Handling the money we have earned is called budgeting. We felt it was important that our children learn to decide in advance what to do with their money rather than having to figure out later where it had all gone. Budgeting their money gives them better control of the resources the Lord has given them.

We taught the children to use a simple budget of ten percent tithe, ten percent savings and eighty percent living expenses. When they got to high school, and college was only four years away, we revised the figures to ten percent tithe, seventy percent savings and twenty percent living. We have friends who let their children (ages seven, nine and thirteen) decide their own ratios. Ratios are not magic, but they do teach children to assess their finances, anticipate their needs, meet obligations and spend their money wisely.

By learning to budget, children become aware of the value of money and the responsibilities of life. I can remember Todd's sad little face when he couldn't buy a soccer ball because, "It isn't in my budget." Through budgeting children learn the cost-effectiveness of life.

Since Tanya and Todd's beginning budgets were so simple, we felt it was important for them to be exposed to the family budget and, as a part of the family, to assume some responsibility for family finances. This helped them see themselves as a part of a whole rather than trying to get what they could for themselves. I know several families who feel children shouldn't know the financial status of the family, but I don't agree. Children do not need to know all the details, but they do need to know that it takes a tremendous amount of money to run a household and that leaving lights on, for example, does make a difference. I know one family who gives the kids a financial update at their "family council" meetings so they can plan together what they can or cannot spend. Those children have become active in the income side of the budget, taking on outside jobs and holding garage sales.

When Tanya was about five, she desperately wanted something we didn't have the money for at the time. To her it was a simple matter of going to the bank and asking for the money. It's hard for children to grasp the fact that our wallets aren't bottomless. When they understand budgeting, they are better able to assume financial responsibility. If you are not accustomed to using a budget yourself, Chapter 13 contains some suggestions.

Knows how to invest money

In an age of IRAs, CDs and money market accounts, we're beginning to see the need of helping children with investments. Investing is the concept of spending to earn.

In other words, you buy a stock to receive its dividends in the same way you might buy a typewriter to type letters for a job. The money spent should be earned back with interest.

Investing is a biblical principle. Jesus reprimanded the servant who hid his talent as a "wicked, lazy slave," while He rewarded the servant who earned a five-fold return.[14] We have talked to the children about different opportunities for investment and the advantages of each. We have also talked about gambling, lotteries and risk taking. In a world of the "fast buck," children need to be taught a balanced approach.

Knows how to save money

Being able to control immediate desires in favor of a future or greater cause is not only a financial principle but a spiritual one. As people of God we sometimes need to put aside immediate desires for eternal values. Financially I'm glad we don't have to think at such a long range, but the principles remain true.

When our children were young, we started with small goals. The children saved for bikes and radios. As they got older, their aspirations grew. We had a goal of each child saving two to three thousand dollars toward college or their careers before they could receive their earned independence. Through budgeting they learned how they could earn and manage their money, and they became more confident about providing for their own needs.

Knows practical how-to's of banking

Banking is a part of our American lifestyle. Instead of chickens we deal in checks. In order to feel confident, our children needed to know how to use a bank — to feel comfortable making deposits and withdrawals, and keeping a checkbook. They also needed to know about the types of savings accounts, about ways of earning interest, and how to read bank statements. We also taught them about the availability of loans and how to establish credit. I have a friend who is so intimidated by banks, she's a nervous wreck whenever she has to deal with one. We wanted our children to know their rights as customers and to be able to deal confidently with banks.

Financial lessons must be reviewed over and over again and are worthless unless applied to daily living. We wanted children who mastered their finances instead of being mastered by them. We wanted children confident in dealing with the world's system without being overcome by it.[15] But most of all we wanted children who were free to honor the, Lord unencumbered by financial matters.[16]

Thought questions

Where do you struggle most in your finances?

How do you think you can keep your children from becoming materialistic?

11

Staying on Course

Your children are not your children.
    They are the sons and daughters of Life's longing for itself.
They come through you but not from you,
And though they are with you yet they belong not to you. . .
You are the bows from which your children as living arrows
    are sent forth.
The archer sees the mark upon the path of the infinite, and
    He bends you with His might
        that His arrows may go swift and far.
Let your bending in the archer's hand be for gladness;
For even as He loves the arrow that flies,
    so He loves also the bow that is stable.

The Prophet

I wonder if you are as overwhelmed as Paul and I felt. Thinking of all the things we needed to develop in our children's lives was enough to make us want to forget the whole matter and go take a nap. But we had so much at stake we knew we had to keep going.

Keeping on target with the plans you have laid may be the most crucial part of the development of your children.

Working on any project, whether building a house or a model airplane, requires the discipline of taking it step by step, piece by piece, working through the manual, following the instructions. And sometimes that doesn't seem very exciting. I know a man who has been working on a model boat for over two years and says it will take him at least that much longer to finish. To me that sounds like forever, and yet I must admit it's a drop in the bucket compared to the time we've spent building our children.

To me, getting started was not half as bad as trying to keep going. That's why it's important to be aware of priorities. Our family is very busy with ministry, sports, jobs, relationships, hobbies and just having fun. I think we would all cease to function if we lost our schedules. But in all our busy-ness, we have tried to hold onto our priorities and let them determine our activity instead of the other way around. When it has come to "family days," time together as a couple or time with the children, we have pushed those priorities to the top of our schedule.

Since consistency was one of our greatest struggles, we tried to view each day as a part of a project with a beginning, an end, and things to do along the way. Periodically we evaluated how we were doing and what changes needed to be made. Looking at our progress in terms of measurable projects helped all of us "hang in there" a little longer when discipline began to falter.

Motivation was the key. As we kept before us the importance of the home in the development of children, Paul and I knew we had no other choice except consistency and discipline if our children were going to be the kind of people we desired them to be before the Lord. Even the secular press reminded us, "The most potent socializing force so far discovered appears to be children learning through observing what others do — particularly parents."[1] This article goes on to say, "Imitating and absorbing the behavior of their parents . . . tends to be more important than the more conscious, deliberate efforts of parents to teach and influence their children."[2]

Joyce Maynard in a *Family Circle* article entitled "Bringing Up Moral Children in This Immoral World," states, "You won't find many books that tell you how to raise good children. You can't sign your son or daughter up for an after-school class in character development. Even Sunday school won't instill a strong spiritual core if the lessons the child learns there are not reinforced the rest of the week at home. Which leaves the task of teaching our children strong values up to us, the parents, even though most of us could use some improvement in the development ourselves. The question is, how to teach them? It begins in the home."[3]

But I especially like how Dr. Albert Schweitzer described the best ways to raise children. He simply said,"There are three ways: by example, by example, by example."[4]

Obviously, our walk had to match our talk. But for us, as for most parents, this is a process and not a qualification with which we entered parenthood. Dr. Bruce Narramore explains, "No one learns to be an effective parent overnight. Being a parent is a long-term educational experience. As long as we have children, we continue to grow."[5] He adds, "There is also an important place for concentrated effort to develop our parental skills. We can improve our familial relations in a few weeks or months if we are willing to invest the time and effort."

No matter how old your children are or where your starting point is in your parenting experience, there is hope. A plan "late in the day" is better than no plan at all. And when I speak of a plan, I don't mean only for the children. You may have to have a plan for your own development in some of the areas we have talked about. I know one parent who went to night school just so he could tutor his son in high school math. Writing your child's Declaration of Independence is up to you. You have the opportunity to look at your child and yourself and determine reasonable goals.

Family days

One of the best things we have done to help maintain consistency in working toward our goals is instituting "family days" — times when we can concentrate on being together as a family, growing with each other and learning to enjoy each other. With Paul's traveling schedule and the children's after-school activities, Sundays have been the best time for us. We sit together in church and then enjoy a leisurely lunch, using the time to catch up on what is important in everyone's life. We often discuss the pastor's sermon or the Sunday school lessons and make practical applications whenever we can.

Then we take time to have some kind of activity for the day. In the ten years we've been having family days, we have come up with almost anything you can think of: hiking, plays, song-fests, Bible studies, books, movies, and trips to the zoo, the beach, the mountains, parks, museums and anywhere else we could think of. The important thing has been being together and communicating.

One house we lived in had a large sliding wooden door that retreated back into the walls. It made a perfect setup for a stage. The children made props and little costumes and acted out their Bible stories. Sometimes they even got us into the act. In their big moment, when the spotlight was on them, they had the opportunity to show us what they had learned and to have fun doing it.

Todd and Tanya also loved reading books. Together we read several missionary biographies like *No Time for Tombstones* and *Peace Child.* But some of their favorite books were *The Chronicles of Narnia* by C. S. Lewis. We read all seven books in the series in just a matter of months. Tanya sat on the floor and colored while she listened; Todd played with his cars. We all enjoyed the books and learned from their analogies.

As the children got older, we began studying Scripture together. This started as a natural outcome of their plays, which became more and more involved. Then we started to talk about their quiet times and the things we were learning in our walks with the Lord. From our journals we shared what the Lord was teaching us. If we had a hard week, we felt free to talk about it and soak up the affirmation of our family. We took our concerns to the Lord in a spirit of oneness.

of oneness.

We also helped Tanya and Todd develop goals for their own lives. We felt part of being independent is knowing where you are going. In 1983 we became familiar with MasterPlanning Associates, which helped us consider questions such as "What are you dreaming of accomplishing 5-20 years from now?" and "What needs do you feel deeply burdened by and uniquely qualified to meet?"[6] We helped our children assess the milestones they had already passed and the ideas they would like to see become reality. We talked about colleges and careers and our purpose in life. Together we were able to dream dreams, some of which have already come true.

As the children became more independent, Paul and I let them organize some of the family days. Each of the four of us planned one Sunday each month. Todd's favorite activity was cross-country skiing; Tanya enjoyed relaxing at Dana Point Harbor.

One of the most practical things we did during our family times was talking about events to come. Each week we got out the calendar, looked at the commitments, and then planned the rest of the week. When the children were little, they were most interested in free time for play; but little by little their activities began to match ours. Looking at the calendar together has helped us take an active interest in one another's lives and avoid the miscommunications which plague busy families. Therefore we were better able to pray for each other and to understand the pressures and opportunities we shared.

Dates

One thing we were sure to put on our calendars was our "date" times. Paul and I tried to spend some time personally with each child every week. For some of you this may seem unrealistic, but keep in mind that whatever amount of time you can put aside to be with your children will be multiplied back to you. We came up with a lot of creative ideas on being together; but the place never seemed to matter as much as the conversation, through which we learned about the children's struggles at school, their attitudes toward sex and their desires to serve the Lord.

Todd and I once had a "date" out on the baseball diamond playing imaginary baseball. I threw an imaginary ball and, as I remember it, Todd hit about six home runs off his imaginary bat. I cheered each one of them. Tanya still talks about the time she and her dad went to the railroad yard to put pennies on the track and watch them get "smushed." Date times were very special times of being together.

Update weekends

Of course, Paul and I didn't want to miss our "date" times either. We knew the importance of that first weekend we spent planning the development of our children. We also knew if we wanted to stay on track, we needed to update our progress and our goals regularly. We tried to get away three times a year for evaluation and relaxation. Sometimes we were lucky enough to put together an out-of-town weekend, but sometimes we just went to a restaurant together. Besides relaxing and enjoying each other, we evaluated how we were doing as a couple, how Tanya and Todd were doing in their Declarations of Independence, what they still needed to know, and in what directions they still needed to develop.

We felt it was very important that we as a couple were united in the way we raised our children. Paul, as head of the family, offered leadership and guidance while I, as the helpmate, offered ideas and suggestions as well as serving as anchor while Paul traveled.

Even though Paul and I worked through our major decisions on our update weekends, we still tried to include the children by bringing information and alternatives to them for their review. I never realized until recently how important it was for them to feel a part of the process. Together we planned cross-country moves. We decided whether we should buy a dog. We checked out the budget, read *Consumer Report,* and trusted the Lord for our needs. We also shared ministry concerns with the children and let them trust the Lord with us for His will. As a result, the ministry was not just Paul and Jeannie's, but the family's.

Sometimes Paul and I included the children in our evaluations. We asked them where they thought their weak points were and what areas they wanted to develop. It gave them a sense of ownership and anticipation as they decided what their next projects would be.

Chapter 13 contains a format we have used in our planning weekends (when we have been fortunate enough to get away). Roger and Donna Vann have written a book, *Secrets of a Growing Marriage,* which is very helpful if you have never done anything like this before. What is important is that you relax, get away from your normal daily pressures and environment, and reflect on all God has given you and wants to do through your lives.

What if it is too late?

Some of you may be sitting there looking at your older teen and thinking, "Well, I've blown it. All this is great but it's just too late." It's never too late. Dr. Bruce Narramore says, "As long as children are in our home, we maintain an influence. It is true that children are more pliable at the first few years of life, but there is plenty of room for change. By starting now, each of us can work for a gratifying family life."[7]

But let's face it, momentum is against us. We may have had the attitude of "come what may" for a long time. Commitment and motivation are major keys to change. As we were writing this book, Paul and I talked about how it needed to be one-fourth information and three-fourths motivation. Information does a person absolutely no good if he is not motivated to act upon it. Ron Dunn has the saying, "Judged by performance, not by knowledge."

We can be motivated by many things. Certainly the Lord motivates us as He impresses us with His will. We challenge you to claim Proverbs 16:3, "Roll your works upon the Lord. Trust also in Him, and He will make your thoughts agreeable to His will, and so shall your plans be established and succeed."[8] We are also motivated by the truth. When we feel in our own hearts something is true, we find courage to pursue it. We challenge you to think about what we have presented in this book, what is true and right for you, and what has been substantiated well enough to motivate you to do it.

We are also motivated by need. Just look at the world around you, and at the lives of "typical teens" as they are portrayed on television. It's a tough world out there, and getting tougher by the minute! The problem often is that parents are not motivated until some critical situation arises, such as a call from the police or the discovery of a teenage pregnancy. Then we sense the need. How much better it is to visualize the child realistically as he begins to develop and to anticipate his needs.

Dr. Narramore encourages us that starting now can produce "immediate dividends in increasing family harmony. It will pay the long-range reward of a happy, fruitful life for our children, and it will pay the lasting dividends of an eternal relationship with God, the Creator of the universe and of the human personality."[9] I love the old saying, "If you aim at nothing, you will hit it every time."

Thought questions

What will keep you from continuing in the plans you have laid out?

When is the best time for you to have family time?

When will be your next "date" with your child? What will you do?

12

How Does it Feel to Fly?

Roll your works upon the Lord —
commit and trust them wholly to Him;
[He will cause your thoughts to become
agreeable to His will, and]
so shall your plans be established
and succeed.

Proverbs 16:3
(Amplified Bible)

The day finally does come when the children leave home, trying out their independence. Tanya and Todd received their Declarations of Independence as seniors in high school. For each it was a proud day with lots of pomp and circumstance. We gave them framed, formal letters of independence as concrete evidence of what they had earned. Tanya hangs her letter on her bedroom wall, and I've seen her reflecting over it. We also gave each child something very tangible (in Tanya's case a gold necklace with 18 beads, in Todd's case a gold engraved pen and pencil set) to remind them of their independence. We also threw a party for each of them so they could celebrate with their friends.

Paul and I are excited about having independent children! It seems that every day we see them grow more while they are out on their own. Our communication has stayed open. Although sometimes there has been a fine line between excitement and fear, we have seen Tanya and Todd make some good decisions based on facts and not on the impulse of the moment.

From the parents' point of view

Giving our children their "wings" has been a little more difficult than I expected. Tanya earned her Declaration of Independence three years ago, and Todd has had his nearly a year. After all our teaching, letting go was a new experience.

Watching them make their own choices was the hardest part of letting go. Sometimes they made good choices, but sometimes not. At times Paul and I were tempted to feel as if the poor choices were our fault. Where had we failed?

But we didn't fail. Oh, sure, I know we made our mistakes. We never claimed to be perfect. But I also know we tried to the best of our abilities to bring Todd and Tanya up in the "knowledge and admonition of the Lord." We have talked and talked about what Scripture means, and we were assured of their knowledge before we gave them their independence. What they did with that knowledge was up to them.

I have to realize, too, that we haven't covered everything. No matter how long it takes to develop a Declaration of Independence, some small matter will slip through the cracks. For Tanya we forgot to teach her to maintain her own checking account. She had learned to balance our checkbook but had never had the responsibility of her own. Later, when she got to college, she didn't realize the responsibility of the daily balancing of an account.

Knowing how to handle these situations is important. No longer can parents rush in and take charge, but they must be sensitive to the young adults. Tanya's checkbook was not my responsibility, but I admitted to her our failure. Then I asked her if she wanted me to help her. (Parents must be careful to offer advice and not just give it.) She chose to have me explain it to her. After we went through how to keep a checkbook, her frustration turned into pride as she gained the confidence to handle it by herself.

When we see our children make unwise choices, our first inclination is to jump right in and try to fix it. But we have to realize they will learn the most from their own experiences. When Todd was younger, I must have told him a hundred times not to jump down the stairs, but it wasn't until he tripped over the dog and broke his leg that he really learned what I was talking about. Experience is the best teacher, but it is also painful. We'd like to teach our children the shortcuts, but sometimes we just can't. These are the times that trusting the LORD becomes so vital.

But trusting the LORD is not easy, and I don't present it as a trite catchall answer for any problem. For me trusting is a day-to-day struggle. Every time I see the children drive out the driveway, I have to commit them to God's care. Letting go of our children tests the depth of our dependence on God. Either He is big enough and caring enough to take care of them, or He is not.

It really has been helpful in my trust of the LORD to review Scripture when my heart has become anxious. Verses like Philippians 4:6,7 remind me, "Be anxious for nothing, but in everything by prayer and supplication with thanksgiving let your requests be made known to God." Then God promises, "And the peace of God, which surpasses all comprehension, shall guard your hearts and your minds in Christ Jesus." I then go on to think about the things I know that are true, honorable, right, pure, lovely (like who God is, how much He cares for my children, what I know they already know, God's promises about them) and let my "mind dwell on these" claiming, "The things you have learned and received and heard and seen in me, practice these things; and the God of peace will be with you."[1]

Psalm 37 also has been an encouragement to me during this period of letting go. Verses 3-7a read,

Trust in the Lord, and do good;
Dwell in the land and cultivate faithfulness.

> Delight yourself in the Lord;
> And He will give you the desires of your heart.
> Commit your way to the Lord, Trust also in Him, and
> He will do it.
> And He will bring forth your righteousness as the light,
> And your judgment as the noonday.
> Rest in the Lord and wait patiently for Him.

There are good promises here, and I claim them often until I can "rest . . . and wait patiently for Him."[2] Then, and only then, can I leave the results of my children's lives up to God.

As parents, you really must consider whether you will be able to let your child go when the time comes. Part of the commitment to start working toward a Declaration of Independence is yours. You commit yourself to love your child unconditionally, to give of your time and energy in planning and helping carry through on the plan, to communicate honestly, and to walk day by day in as godly a manner as you can. You must also commit yourself to let go when the time comes. If you don't, you will set up a standard of mistrust, of not keeping your word, which will be extremely hard to repair. That's why it's important to trust the LORD with your child and rest confidently in His will.

From the child's point of view

From the child's point of view, flying is wonderful, yet scary. Since both of our children are "out of the nest," we thought you might enjoy peeking in on an interview we had with them as we were writing this book.

Question: Can you remember when your parents first approached you with the idea of working toward "earned independence"?

What were some of your initial thoughts?

Todd's response:

Yes, it was in the summer of 1977, when my father took me on a deep-sea fishing trip with his directors. One morning when everyone split up to have their quiet times, my dad told me about their plan; and I thought it was really neat. I knew that with parents like mine, I definitely was going to be different from all my friends, especially with all the different interesting experiences I've had. Dad had a lot of neat ideas, and I realized they were going to make me more mature and build characteristics in my life that many of my friends might never have — or if they had them, they probably would not be brought into their lives until they were much older.

Tanya's response:

I thought it sounded pretty neat. I am very "organizationally oriented," and the plan was all in a very organized manner that interested me. I thought it would be neat to accomplish goals that way and to be able to check them off the list.

Question: Looking at some of your friends at school, do you think your Declaration of Independence has helped you be better prepared for life?

Tanya's response:

I think I handle being on my own a lot better than my friends do. For example, I know how to handle money, even though sometimes I make mistakes and don't spend my money wisely.

I've also been very conscientious about the priorities in my life, more so than my friends are. Whether or not I followed through on them exactly, I still knew my priorities; and I think I came out better in the long run by working at them. I think it made me more ready to cope with not having my parents around. I don't have to look toward my parents and say, "Oh, help me out of this situation," but I can just ask their advice as people.

Todd's response:

The Declaration of Independence, I think, has definitely changed my life. Its effects have already made me different from my friends. I've been in situations with my friends where I think I have been able to handle myself better than they did simply because of the experiences I've had. During my freshman year our drama club went to Los Angeles to the Spaghetti Factory and to a nice play; and I was comfortable in that situation just because my parents had taught me how to handle myself in a nice restaurant.

My parents have given me a good model to follow. I've seen the respect my father shows my mother; so when I date I know how to go about seating the girl at a table or opening a door for her — just respecting her. Some of my friends don't know how to handle these situations.

Question: In your own words, how do you think other parents approach the raising of their children?
Todd's response:

I think a lot of my friends, even some who are Christians, have parents who just kind of set down the guidelines and say, "This is how it is — no ifs, ands or buts." And the parents don't really take time to ask what the children think on certain issues — "Do you agree with what your father and I have to say on this?" for instance. When our family is making a decision, or when my parents have a thought about something, they'll bring it to my sister and me and say, "Well, what do you think about this?"
Tanya's response:

I've seen a lot of different approaches. I've seen some parents who tell their kids everything to do and don't let their kids make their own decisions or help make family decisions. Everything is decided for them. I know some kids in my dorm who were raised that way. Now they can't make good decisions; they work a lot on feelings and not on facts.

For instance, I have a friend who decided to leave school and go back home because she had a boyfriend there. She wouldn't apply for any state grants or any money from the school because she didn't think she was coming back. She just wanted to be back home with her parents and her boyfriend. Now she really regrets doing it because it didn't work out. Her decision was all based on emotions she had one weekend instead of on a lot of prayerful consideration or time to contemplate the pros and cons of the situation. Besides, she's having an extremely hard time trying to live with her parents again after being on her own last year.

Question: How does this differ from your parents' approach?
Tanya's response:

My parents have made a lot of decisions for me and yet have made me make a lot of decisions. They have given me freedom when I've show I can handle it responsibly — and even when I haven't been responsible, just to let me know I'm an individual who has worth and importance. I know now that I am quite intelligent and I can make decisions. Later on I will become responsible in certain areas that I might not be doing well in right now.

Todd's response:

As I look back, I know my parents have really cared about our lives and what we've been interested in. They haven't said, "Kids, we're going to do this because your father and I want to do this," or anything like that.
father and I want to do this," or anything like that.

They consulted us about activities we wanted. We spent at least an hour or two doing something with our parents each weekend — different kinds of activities that kids usually do. My dad and I got a little airplane that we put fuel into, and we held it by a string as it flew around in the air. We also got interested in train sets and spent some of our activity time on them. That was really fun! I know most of my friends' parents never took time for special activities with them; so I feel that really shows my parents' interest in my life.

Question: What results do you see from other approaches?
Todd's response:

I think a lot of my friends have kind of fallen apart. Even Christian kids with Christian parents (if the parents didn't spend a lot of time with them) are wasting their lives, partying all the time, into poor groups of kids at school, and so on. It seems like the kids are saying, "My parents don't care about me; so I don't really care what I do." I think that attitude is pretty sad.

And a lot of my friends don't feel they can talk to their parents. I feel that my parents are two of my good friends, but a lot of my friends see their parents not as friends but as rulers.

Tanya's response:

I just think that a lot of kids have to struggle in many areas that I don't have to struggle in. I think I've matured a lot quicker than they have. It helps to have parents see a child as an individual and a friend, a responsible person who can make decisions on his own and can live independently.

Question: Was there ever a time when you resented the concept of the Declaration of Independence?

Tanya's response:

Yes. Part of the second semester of my freshman year. I think I was just being rebellious and didn't feel like following any authority. I just didn't want much to do with God or anything like that. Sometimes I felt as if independence was being held over my head — "If you're not good, you won't get it"; but I worked through it. It was just a growing period in my life, and I learned a lot from it. I learned just how much I needed to learn and how faithful my parents really are to me.

Todd's response:

No, I don't think I ever resented the Declaration of Independence. I can remember a few times, when I had to read some books or memorize some verses, that I thought, "Man alive! I'd much rather go out and play ball with the guys in the street." Then after a while I decided the Declaration really was a good deal. So I don't think I've really resented it, but there have been some times I didn't want to work at it just because I was too lazy.

Question: Do you think it has been good for Tanya (Todd)?

Todd's response:

Yes. She knows how to pump gas. I guess that sounds funny, but some girls don't have any idea how to pump gas or even where the gas cap is on the car, which is sad. Tanya knows how to change a tire and check the oil and the tire pressure. So she's learned some things she really needs to know but might not have known without the Declaration of Independence.

Tanya's response:

Yes. I haven't seen Todd much this last year, but I can see he's matured a lot. He's not as giddy or wild as he used to be. When somebody tells him to calm down or respond in a cooler manner or act more mature, he knows how to change. I can relate to him better as a friend instead of as a little brother who's still a pest sometimes.

Question: Do you know young people who are exceptionally dependent? How has it affected their lives?

Tanya's response:

One person who is very dependent is _____ . Her father died about two years ago, and she and her mother are like best friends. During the time she was at school, she went home every weekend and was constantly on the phone to her mother. I don't think she could handle being away from her mother. I think they're extremely dependent on each other, and they can't handle life without each other. It's extremely stifling.

One of my friends lived overseas, and she did not know how to do anything — clean a room, do laundry. She didn't know how to do anything other than dress herself and study. Her roommates had to help her constantly to keep her out of trouble. She didn't know how to manage her money or her time; her parents just hadn't taught her. I think that's too dependent.

Todd's response:

One guy I know has great parents, but they've never taught him to handle himself socially. He's really obnoxious, and I don't think he could handle a situation where he had

to take charge and act properly. He hasn't had the opportunity
to develop those abilities, which I think is sad.

Other powerful statements:
Tanya

When you're independent, you have to have the ability
to give up things whether you want to or not. I find that
dependent people don't want to give up anything; they want
to have it all, and they can't. Having everything doesn't
cause any maturity.

When you're dependent, it hurts you as an individual
because you feel insecure, feel like you can't handle things,
and feel bad about yourself. You don't have past successes
to say, "If I did this in the past, I can do this in the future."

Being dependent also hurts your family relationships because your parents are not going to be totally secure about
trusting you if they don't feel you can handle whatever
comes along.

When you're dependent you have a tendency to compare
yourself with others. That just adds to your insecurity and
your feeling like you have to have others help you all the time.
Todd:

I think my sister and I have always been pretty independent.
While we were in China we didn't travel in the same group
as our parents or live with them. The last two summers
I've been totally independent in China, traveling with a
group, and I've been able to handle situations adequately.
My parents have just been exceptional in teaching me how
to behave in different situations, and not to be obnoxious.
Of course there is a time and a place to goof off, but you
need to know when that's appropriate.

One of the most fun family days I can remember was at
Easter break in 1976 or 1977 when our family went to the
little town of Cripple Creek, Colorado. On the day that
stands out in my mind, we hiked to some of the old gold
mines and poked around there. We knocked around and
looked at the little old mine shafts and the decrepit little
shacks the miners stayed in. I found an old mining pan that

was really neat. We also looked at some property we thought might be fun to own and to build a little cabin on.

We went fishing that day, and somebody had told us that the best bait for trout was grasshoppers. So I remember my dad and I were running all over a big open field, diving through the weeds, catching the grasshoppers that were bouncing all over the place, and putting them into jars and bags.

In the spiritual area, having a consistent quiet time, memorizing verses, and reading different books have been special to me. I've especially liked *Preparing for Adolescence* and *Pursuit of Holiness.* They've given me goals I know most of my friends don't have. I've read a few of Josh's [Josh McDowell's] books, and I've traveled with Josh, which has built good characteristics into my life — seeing how he lives, traveling with him, hearing his talks. Even when I've heard the same talk five or six times, I still get something different out of it every time.

Just knowing how to look through the Bible when I want to know about a certain subject has been good. I've learned to use a Bible dictionary or an exhaustive concordance or just the concordance in the back of the Bible to find out what I want to know.

Taking off

So there they go. And as your children leave, I want to congratulate you as their parents. Raising children is one of life's hardest jobs, and raising children who know and love the LORD in an ungodly world is even more difficult. But you have done it. You have fought the fight. You have kept the faith. You have sacrificed your time and effort. You have persevered.

Jeremiah has some interesting verses about sheep, and I can't help feeling they apply to the raising of our children. Jeremiah 17:16 says, "But as for me, I have not hurried away from being a shepherd after Thee." Being a shepherd is not a "fun" job. It involves a lot of wandering around, guiding, protecting — in fact, it can get downright boring. But just as God has not hurried away from being our shepherd, neither should we hurry away from our responsibilities as parents. Sure, there are other things out there calling to us — money to be earned, miles to be traveled, flattering degrees, promotions and social standing to be sought — but none are more important than our sheep. One day the Lord may ask us, "Where is the flock that was given you, your beautiful sheep?"[13]

Psalm 71:17-20 has a powerful message we would like to leave with you.

> O God, Thou has taught me from my youth;
>   And I still declare Thy wondrous deeds.
> And even when I am old and gray,
>   Oh God, do not forsake me,
> Until I declare Thy strength to this generation,
>   Thy power to all who are to come.
> For Thy righteousness, O God,
>   Reaches to the heavens,
> Thou who hast done great things;
>   O God, who is like Thee?

Thought questions

What are the concerns and dreams of your childen?

How can you help them see their dreams accomplished?

What effective "shepherding" techniques have you used in your family? Take time to thank the Lord for each one.

13

Resources and Worksheets

Developing your child's Declaration of Independence is not an easy matter. It takes thought and reflection to decide what your child needs and how to develop it. We have included some worksheets and resources to help the process along, but in no way are they meant to be complete. In fact, in some of the areas we have left blanks for you to fill in. These are exactly what we have called them — worksheets. Cross out; add to; wear them out with use.

The summary sheet is a bird's eye view of the areas we have dealt with in the book. In situations where you may want to make a quick evaluation, it will save you from having to flip pages.

Some of the worksheets have other information with them. For example, the worksheet on intellectual development includes a list of classics. The financial worksheet has some budgeting ideas. We encourage you to use these sheets to augment your personal information.

The resource list is a combination of the suggested readings at the end of the worksheets, a bibliography from the footnotes and references we have used, and other resources we felt may be beneficial to you.

We hope these will help you. We are open to any comments or suggestions you may have. Feel free to contact us through Here's Life Publishers.

Summary

Spiritual
— knows how to study the Bible
— experiences a consistent "quiet time" with the LORD
— has a general working knowledge of Scripture
— is developing as a person of faith including
    knows how to seek the Lord
    is memorizing Scripture
    is faithful in obedience
— has a strong concept of who God is
— has a strong understanding of who he is in Christ
— is consistently growing in the ministry of the Holy Spirit
— is a person of prayer

Physical
— accepts himself physically as a gift from God
— understands and practices personal hygiene
— maintains proper weight for his age
— keeps a regular physical fitness program
— maintains a good diet
— has at least one sport to develop in
— has regular medical check-ups
— maintains a good appearance
— has a biblical perspective of sex

Intellectual
— has working knowledge of basic academic skills
— has read 20 world classics
— has general grasp of world history and current events
— knows how to find needed information
— knows how machines work
— knows how to drive
— has a practical knowledge of general skills
— is developing creatively
— knows intellectually the "whys" of his belief
— is teachable

— knows and uses principles of time management
— has a sense of ethics

Social
— understands the biblical motivation for relationships
— takes responsibility, as part of society, for its actions
— is confident in the role of host, hostess or guest
— knows common etiquette and courtesies
— is confident in making introductions
— is able to relate to various age groups
— puts others at ease because he is at ease

Emotional
— has a sense of significance as a person
— has a sense of belonging
— is accepting of others
— is able to make decisions
— understands, makes and carries through on commitments
— is able to have fun and enjoy life
— is able to communicate his feelings to others
— is able to give emotionally to others
— is able to handle emotionally difficult situations

Financial
— has a biblical perspective of finances
— has a giving heart
— knows how to work
— understands how to manage finances
— knows how to invest money
— knows how to save money
— knows practical how-to's of banking

WORKSHEET FOR CHAPTER 5

1. Knows how to study the Word of God
— recognizes the importance of studying the Bible
— knows and uses Bible study techniques
— keeps a Bible notebook
— makes significant insights and applications
— knows how to use study tools such as
 dictionary
 Bible dictionary
 concordance
 cross references
 maps
 topical Bibles
 translations
 devotional guides and workbooks
— has a balance between using study guides and digging for himself
— is confident about participating when the family studies together

2. Experiences a consistent "quiet time" with the LORD
— recognizes the importance of a time with the LORD
— has seen his parents spend time with the LORD
— keeps a quiet-time notebook
— has a regular time and place to meet with the LORD
— is showing creativity and growth in his time with the LORD
— is developing his own motivation and conviction for his quiet time
— is willing to share his insights with others

3. Has a general working knowledge of Scripture
— knows the books of the Bible and their order
— knows the chronological order of the books and the major divisions of Scripture
— knows the authorship and historical background of the books

— knows the general themes of Scripture and how they
  are developed

4. Is developing as a person of faith
— knows how to seek the Lord
— uses Scripture to confirm and build his faith
— has memorized passages which build his faith
— trusts God in his personal life
— knows what it means and is able to "give thanks in
  all things"
— has memorized James 1:2-8 (Phillips Translation)

5. Has a strong concept of who God is
— knows the attributes of God
— has memorized passages which build his image of God
— has read *Knowledge of the Holy* by A. W. Tozer
— has a feel for who God is and how He relates to individuals
— can see God reflected through nature
— recognizes the character of God at work in his own life

6. Has a strong understanding of who he is in Christ
— has a strong understanding of God's unconditional
  acceptance
— understands what God has done for him
— understands the sin nature of man
— has received Christ as his personal Savior
— recognizes his need for relationships within the body
  of Christ
— has read *His Image . . . My Image*

7. Is consistently growing in the ministry of the Holy Spirit
— understands who the Holy Spirit is and how He ministers through a life
— walks in the Spirit, giving the control of his life over
  to Him
— understands "spiritual breathing" and the forgiveness
  of sins

— knows how to share his faith in the power of the
   Holy Spirit, leaving the results up to God
— exhibits the fruit of the Spirit
— is open to the leading of the Holy Spirit for direction
   in his life

8. Is a person of prayer
— understands what prayer is
— feels free to express himself in his prayer life
— consistently and spontaneously communicates with
   God
— is confident praying with others
— uses a prayer notebook

Suggested passages for memorization
Salvation:

John 1:12	Romans 5:8
John 3:16	Romans 6:23
John 10:10	Ephesians 2:8,9
John 14:6	Hebrews 13:5
Romans 3:23	Revelation 3:20

Ministry of the Holy Spirit:

Matthew 5:6	Galatians 5:22,23
John 14:16,17	Ephesians 5:18
John 15:5	2 Peter 1:9
Acts 1:8	1 John 1:9
1 Corinthians 2:14,15	1 John 5:14,15
1 Corinthians 3:1-3	

Others include:

Hebrews 12:1-3	1 Corinthians 13:4-10 (Living)
James 1:2-6 (Phillips)	Philippians 1:27-29
Philippians 1:27-29	Colossians 1:28,29
Philippians 4:6,7	Matthew 28:19-21
Psalm 23	Isaiah 40:28-31
Isaiah 41:8-12	Joshua 1:7,8
Psalm 37:1-8	Psalm 37:23-24

Suggested reading
  Doorways to Discipleship, Winkie Pratney
  Knowledge of the Holy, A. W. Tozer
  Personal Bible Study Notebook, John Souter

WORKSHEET FOR CHAPTER 6

1. **Accepts himself physically as a gift from God**
   — understands the act of personal creation
   — has read *His Image . . . My Image*

2. **Understands and practices personal hygiene**
   — understands the reasoning behind good hygiene
   — is aware of body functions and their development
   — practices good hygiene as listed below:

   _____

   _____

   _____

   _____

   _____

3. **Maintains proper weight for his age**
   — knows his proper weight
   — knows the medical benefits of not being overweight

4. **Keeps a regular physical fitness program**
   — has chosen some form of exercise
   — keeps a regular physical fitness program

5. **Maintains a good diet**
   — knows the basic food groups
   — knows the benefits of eating well
   — is able to control his eating habits
   — has a diet low in sugar, cholesterol, salt and fats, high
      in fiber with adequate protein

6. **Has at least one sport to develop in**
   — has chosen a sport to work on
   — is developing coordination
   — is developing team relationships

7. Has regular medical checkups
— physical examination once a year
— dental checkups twice a year
— eye exam once every two years
— feels free to see a doctor when the occasion arises

8. Maintains a good appearance
— understands the importance of a good appearance
— feels free to get advice from "experts" in areas of need
— is aware of fashions
— dresses appropriately
— understands real beauty is internal

9. Has a biblical perspective on sex
— understands the biblical perspective of sex
— has read the following books and discussed them with
    parents:
        Almost Twelve
        Preparing for Adolescence
        The Stork Is Dead
— is developing his own convictions about sex
— feels free to talk with parents and other respected
    adults about sex
— recognizes the results of sexual sin
— realizes the emotional pull "being in love" has on
    convictions
— has made a list of reasons why he personally wants to
    wait until after marriage to enjoy sex
— has read *Passion and Purity* by Elizabeth Elliot

Suggested reading
The Stork Is Dead, Charlie W. Shedd
Preparing for Adolescence, Dr. James Dobson
Almost Twelve, Kenneth Taylor

Worksheet for Chapter 7

1. **Has working knowledge of basic academic skills**
   — is proficient in reading, writing and arithmetic
   — has positive feelings about learning and his schoolwork
   — keeps abreast of homework and grades

2. **Has read twenty world classics**
   — has chosen books from the "Classics" list
   — is reading approximately four books each year

3. **Has general grasp of world history and current events**
   — understands the importance of history on current events
   — understands the basic issues and activities of current events
   — knows the names of local and national government officials

4. **Knows how to find needed information**
   — knows how to use a library card catalogue
   — knows where different types of books are found
   — knows how to use reference materials such as
       dictionaries
       encyclopedias
       thesaurus
       Readers' Guide to Periodicals
   — knows what other resources (films, records, painting, etc.) are available at his local library

5. **Knows how machines work**

6. **Knows how to drive**
   — has taken driver's education through school
   — takes driving seriously
   — knows how to do simple maintenance on the family car
   — is financially responsible for gas, insurance and other auto expenses

7. Has a practical knowledge of general skills
— has basic household skills of
cooking and meal preparation
menu selection and shopping
washing and ironing clothes
cleaning
stain removal
sewing
room arrangements and interior decorating
taking care of lawn and gardens

_____

_____

_____

— knows how to do simple household jobs such as
unclogging a drain
unplugging a toilet
replacing a fuse
gluing broken parts
hanging pictures and curtains
carpentry repairs
electrical repairs
— organizes and cares for his tools

8. Is developing creatively
— has some creative outlet
— realizes creativity and artistic ability are not the same

9. Knows intellectually the "whys" of his belief
— has read *Know Why You Believe*
— is secure in the intellectual foundation of his faith
— is able to defend his faith

10. Is teachable

11. Knows and uses principles of management
— knows how to plan and uses his time effectively
— recognizes the need for relaxation

— has a personal filing system
— is usually on time

12. Has a sense of personal ethics
— has read *In His Steps* and discussed the principle of "being like Jesus"
— has developed personal convictions on what he would or would not do in situations and has demonstrated these convictions through role-playing
— is able to hold on to his convictions under pressure
— is careful about judging others whose stand differs from his

LIST OF CLASSICS*

Old favorites and classics

Jane Eyre, Bronte
Wuthering Heights, Bronte
Robinson Crusoe, Defoe
David Copperfield, Dickens
Great Expectations, Dickens
The Lost World, Doyle
The Three Musketeers, Gilbreth
The Legend of Sleepy Hollow, Irving

Captains Courageous, Kipling
Kim, Kipling
Kipling Stories, Kipling
Chucklebait, Scoggin
Kidnapped, Stevenson
Treasure Island, Stevenson
Gulliver's Travels, Swift
Around the World in 80 Days, Verne
20,000 Leagues Under the Sea, Verne

Very highly recommended

Sounder, Armstrong
Tree of Freedom, Caudill
Johnny Tremain, Forbes
My Side of the Mountain, George
Old Yeller, Gipson
Adam of the Road, Gray

Jazz Country, Heptoff
Smoky, The Cowhorse, James
Rifles for Watie, Keith
From the Mixed-up Files of Mrs. Basil E. Frankweiler, Konigsburg

Carry On, Mr. Bowditch, Latham
Island of the Blue Dolphins, O'Dell
It's Like This, Cat, Neville
The Yearling, Rawlings
Onion John, Shimin
The Witch of Blackbird Pond, Speare
Juan de Pareja, de Trevino
Shadow of a Bull, Wojciechowska

Recommended

Born Free, Adamson
Only Yesterday, Allen
White Falcon, Arnold

Henry III, Krumgold
The Rock and the Willow, Lee
The Skating Rink, Lee

National Velvet, Bagnold
Watch for a Tall White Sail, Bell
The Strange Intruder, Catherall
Santiago, Clark
Legends of the North, Coolidge
Tree House Island, Corbett
Silent World, Causteau

Fast Man on a Pivot, Decker
The Coriander, Dillon
I, Adam, Fritz
Southtown, Graham
Mythology, Hamilton
The House of the Nies, Hamilton
Dangerous Journey, Hamori
Kon-Tiki, Heyerdahl
The Outsiders, Hinton
Up a Road Slowly, Hunt
Fofana, Guillot
Edge of Two Worlds, Jones
The Year of the Raccoon, Kingman

The Rough Road, MacPherson
Kirsti, Miller
Lost Queen of Egypt Morrison
The Black Joke, Mowat
Rascal, North
Sea Fever, Peyton
*Tales and Poems of
    Edgar Allan Poe*, Poe
Beowulf, Sutcliff
Voyage of the Vagabond, Thruelsen
The Hobbit, Tolkien
Good-Bye to the Jungle, Townsend
The Singing Tree, Seredy
Splintered Sword, Treece
Huckleberry Finn, Twain
Tom Sawyer, Twain
The Dream Watcher, Wersba

Especially for Junior High

Little Women, Alcott
Watch for a Tall White Sail, Ball
Junior Miss, Benson
Going on Sixteen, Cavanna
Jean and Johnny, Cleary
Three Who Met, Craig
Seventeenth Summer, Daly
The Popular Crowd, Emery

Big Doc's Girl, Meadiris
Ready or Not, Stolz
To Tell Your Love, Stolz
Who Wants Music on Monday, Stolz
Cress Delahanty, West
Sparrow Lake, York
The Ghost of the Isherwoods, York

Sports

The Kid Who Batted 1,000, Allison
Quarterback and Son, Archibald
Patch, Frick
All-Pro Quarterback, Friendlich
Full Court Press, Friendlich
The Long Green, Gault
No Head For Soccer, Harkins

Powerhouse Five, Herman
Breakway Back, Hutto
All American, Tunis
Go Team Go, Tunis
High Pockets, Tunis
Yea, Wild Cats, Tunis

Animal stories

Far Voice Calling, Adair
National Velvet, Bagnold
The Incredible Journey, Burnfold
Good-bye Kate, Clark
Black Stallion, Farley
Old Yeller, Gipson

The Call of the Wild, London
The Pond, Murphy
Rascal, North
Green Grass of Wyoming, O'Hara
The Yearling, Rawlings
Old Ramon, Schafer

Smoky the Cow Horse, James
Lassie Come Home, Knight

Goodbye, My Lady, Street

Foreign stories

More Than Courage, Baudeus
The Ark, Benary-Isbert
Bowan Farm, Benary-Isbert
Jamie, Bennett
The Big Loop, Bishop
Santiago, Clark
Ring the Judas Bell, Forman
East to Freedom, Fukei
Fofana, Guillot

Francie, Hahn
As a May Morning, Hogarth
First the Lightning, Knight
To Beat a Tiger, Lewis
Flowers of Hiroshima, Morris
Annuzza, Seuberlich
Old Mali and the Box, Sherman
North to Freedom, Holm

Science fiction

R Is for Rocket, Bradbury
Dolphin Island, Clearke
Outpost of Jupiter, Del Rey
Farmer in the Sky, Heinlein
Podkane of Mars, Heinlein
The Rolling Stones, Heinlein
A Wrinkle in Time, L'Engle

Key Cut of Time, Norton
The X Factor, Norton
Star Surgeon, Nourse
The Universe Between, Nourse
20,000 Leagues Under the Sea, Verne

Other interesting selections

Broken Arrow, Arnold
The Faraway Lurs, Behn
Banners at Shenandoah, Catton
The Far-Off Land, Claudill
Spy in Old Detroit, Emery
April Morning, Fast
Johnny Tremain, Forbes
Across Five Aprils, Hunt

Komantcia, Keith
Rifles for Watie, Keith
The Foreigner, Malvern
Thunderbolt House, Pease
The Bronze Bow, Speare
The Witch of Blackbird Pond, Speare

* Books were on a recommended reading list from the Clearwater Public Library, Clearwater, Florida. They were recommended for junior high age and up. We do not personally recommend each and every book but advise parents to be aware of what their children are reading.

Suggested reading

Honey for a Child's Heart, Gladys Hunt
Why You Believe, Paul Little
Evidence That Demands a Verdict, Josh McDowell

WORKSHEET FOR CHAPTER 8

1. **Understands the biblical motivation for relationships**
   — understands his responsibility to represent Christ to others
   — is secure in his relationship with Christ
   — is secure in his relationship within the family
   — has good peer relationships
   — is developing relationships outside of peergroup

2. **Has taken responsibility, as a part of society, for its actions**
   — participates in group activities
   — is able to confront a group when he feels his integrity is being violated
   — does not avoid taking responsibility for his part of group activities (good and bad)
   — has an interest in political issues
   — feels his responsibility as a citizen of his country
   — shows personal responsibility in his actions when adults are not around

3. **Is confident in the role of host, hostess or guest**
   — has an understanding of the goal of entertaining
   — is sensitive to the needs of others
   — thinks creatively how to best meet those needs
   — recognizes his own needs and how to meet them
   — follows through on entertaining
   — knows how to have a formal event
   — knows how to entertain casually
   — is comfortable as a guest
   — knows how to receive or reject an invitation
   — is faithful in communicating appreciation after an event

4. **Knows common etiquette and courtesies**
   — knows and practices common courtesies such as:

   _____

   _____

_____

_____

_____

— understands the reasoning behind being courteous
— understands and practices good dating etiquette

5. Is confident in making introductions
— knows how to make proper introductions
— is confident in using the phone
— knows how to handle nuisance calls

6. Is able to relate to various age groups

— is confident relating to adults
— is confident relating to elderly people
— is confident relating to children
— is confident relating to individuals from differing cultural backgrounds

7. Puts others at ease because he is at ease
— enjoys being with people
— is a person others enjoy being with

Suggested reading
Miss Manners' Guide to Rearing Perfect Children, Judith Martin
Too Big to Spank, Jay Kesler
Between Parent and Teenager, Haim Ginott

WORKSHEET FOR CHAPTER 9

1. Has a sense of significance as a person
— is growing in his ability to identify his feelings
— is able to "own" his emotions and take responsibility for them
— knows of God's acceptance for him
— is secure in his parents' acceptance
— receives the advice of others, processes it in light of his integrity and Scripture, and draws his own conclusion from it
— has a feel for the emotional aspects of God
— understands the difficulty in accepting emotions (i.e., sin, fear of rejection, societal norms, fear of consequences, etc.) and how to process emotions
— has a sense of personal integrity

2. Has a sense of belonging
— has a sense of family identity
— accepts love from his family and is affectionate
— has a sense of being part of the "family of God"
— enjoys family traditions

3. Is accepting of others
— is open to people from other countries and cultures
— works to receive people he would not naturally gravitate toward
— can identify with the feelings of others and understand emotionally their point of view
— respects others even if he does not agree with them
— is flexible in dealing with others

4. Is able to make decisions

— understands the emotional difficulty in making decisions
— understands and uses the "sound-mind" principle
— understands the ministry of the Holy Spirit in decision making

— is aware of the "aftershocks" of decisions
— is secure enough to make decisions outside of confor-
    mity

5. Understands, makes and carries through on commit-
   ments
— is willing to make commitments
— takes commitments seriously
— is faithful to his commitments
— knows how to back out of commitment if it becomes
    necessary
— is not afraid to make commitments in relationships

6. Is able to have fun and enjoy life
— understands the emotional, physical and spiritual ben-
    efits of fun and relaxation
— seems to be free to laugh and "cut up" when it is ap-
    propriate
— gives himself space in his schedule for fun
— can put aside his natural desire for fun when the cir-
    cumstances demand it (i.e., proper decorum in
    church, attention to schoolwork, etc.)

7. Is able to communicate his feelings to others
— seems confident in communicating to others
— feels as if he has something to offer
— understands the two levels of communication
— is growing in his ability to "read between the lines"
    and identify the emotional level of conversations
— is confident in communicating on the emotional level

8. Is able to give emotionally to others
— has confidence in and understanding of who he is and
    what the LORD has done within his life
— recognizes the needs of others and desires to meet them
— is growing in his wisdom of how to meet the needs of
    others
— does not entangle himself in unhealthy relationships

9. Is able to handle emotionally difficult situations
— is able to identify his feelings and separate them from
    the feelings of others
— is able to process his feelings to see if they are related
    to other things (i.e., feelings he's had before, fears
    of the future, jealousy, etc.)
— is able to objectify his feelings and view them in light
    of Scripture and other accurate information
— is responsible for actions prompted by his emotions
— comes to the point of peace within himself and with
    God

Principles of God's love
1. God created me to receive and respond to His love.

     John 15:9,15   John 17:23
     Isaiah 43:1,4   Isaiah 62:4,5

2. God's love is eternal and unconditional.

     Jeremiah 31:3   1 John 4:19
     Romans 8:38,39

3. God loved me enough to die for and forgive my sins.

     2 Corinthians 5:21   1 John 4:10
     Isaiah 63:9   Hebrews 10:12,17
     Romans 8:1,33,34   Galatians 5:1,6,13

4. I belong to God's family.

     1 John 3:1   Romans 8:14-17,32

5. God thinks about me and watches over me.

     1 Peter 5:7   Psalm 139:17-18
     Psalm 32:8   Psalms 33:18 and 34:15
     Deuteronomy 7:9   Matthew 6:34
     Psalm 111:5   Isaiah 49:15,16
     Zephaniah 3:17

6. He will give only the best to me.

     Romans 8:28-32   Psalm 139:16b
     Psalm 23   Psalm 37
     Ephesians 3:20   Romans 12:2
     Jeremiah 29:11   Isaiah 46:10,11
     Deuteronomy 1:30-33

7. He will meet my every need.

Romans 8:32	Matthew 6:32,33
Matthew 7:7-11	Mark 10:29,30
1 Timothy 6:17	Philippians 4:19
Psalm 37	

Suggested reading

His Image . . . My Image, Josh McDowell

Christian Child-Rearing and Personality Development, Paul Meier

Hide and Seek, James Dobson

Worksheet for Chapter 10

1. **Has a biblical perspective of finances**
   — understands that everything comes from God
   — has a spirit of thankfulness for what he has
   — is familiar with biblical principles of finances
   — is aware of the control of materialism and envy
   — knows and practices the principle of tithing

2. **Has a giving heart**
   — gives cheerfully, sacrificially, and consistently
   — is sensitive to the Holy Spirit in his giving
   — takes part in at least one worthwhile, selfless, giving project each year

3. **Knows how to work**
   — is a contented laborer
   — is faithful in his jobs
   — has pride in his work
   — works to earn money from others
   — is confident in communicating with his boss

4. **Understands how to manage finances**
   — knows how to make wise financial decisions
   — uses a simple budget
   — understands the family budget

5. **Knows how to invest money**
   — understands the principles behind investing
   — has a basic understanding of various kinds of investments and how to use them
   — makes wise investments which pay off in good returns

6. **Knows how to save money**
   — is able to save money
   — saves for special purchases
   — has saved two thousand dollars toward college or a career

— is aware of scholarships available and how to apply
   for them

7. Knows practical how-to's of banking
   — has and keeps his own checking account
   — uses a savings account
   — knows how to take out a loan and establish credit
   — knows the benefits and dangers of credit cards
   — knows how to read bank statements
   — is confident dealing with financial institutions

Principles of Budgeting

The family budget

1. Establish categories such as:
   — clothing   — emergency fund
   — entertainment   — house payment/rent
   — improvements/repairs   — insurance
   — investments/savings   — medical
   — miscellaneous/   — utilities (gas, electricity,
        petty cash   water, phone,
   — gifts   garbage, etc.)
   — auto expenses   — groceries
   — tithe   — other

   See Budget Worksheet at the end of this explanation.

2. Consider "working money" — the amount you have left
   after taxes and other deductions are taken out.

Example:	Gross income	$1,600 per month
	Less taxes	160
	Working money	$1,440

3. Assign a priority ranking to each category (1,2,3,etc.).

4. Assign a money amount to each category, subtracting it
   from your working money as you go.

Example:

	Working money		$1,440
	#1-tithe	$160	1,280
	#2-house/rent	400	880
	#3-utilities	100	780

If you have trouble deciding how much to put into each category, *The Financial Planning Workbook* has percentage quotients which may help.

5. Assign each category to the proper pay period.

Example: First pay period	- rent, one-half groceries, tithe
Second pay period	- utilities, one-half groceries, clothes

Another way would be to take out a percentage for each category for each pay period.

6. Enter all funds on a master sheet.

Example:

Date	Entry	Credit	Debit	Balance
11/2/81	paycheck	$720		$720
11/2/81	clothing		$20	700
11/2/81	groceries		75	625

You may want to use the Budget Master Account sheets at the end of this section or purchase a ledger book to record your figures.

7. Transfer figures to category sheets.
Work off category sheets rather than your checkbook to see what money is available.

Example:

Category: Clothing

Date	Entry	Credit	Debit	Balance
11/02/81	paycheck	$50		$ 50
11/17/81	paycheck	50		100
11/19/81	shoes		$15	85

You may want to use the Category Account sheets or a ledger.

Budget Worksheet — for categories

Priority #	Category	Amount	Pay Period

Budget Master Account

Date	Entry	Credit	Debit	Balance

Category Account for _____

Date	Entry	Credit	Debit	Balance
____	_____	_____	_____	_____
____	_____	_____	_____	_____
____	_____	_____	_____	_____
____	_____	_____	_____	_____
____	_____	_____	_____	_____
____	_____	_____	_____	_____
____	_____	_____	_____	_____
____	_____	_____	_____	_____
____	_____	_____	_____	_____
____	_____	_____	_____	_____
____	_____	_____	_____	_____
____	_____	_____	_____	_____
____	_____	_____	_____	_____
____	_____	_____	_____	_____
____	_____	_____	_____	_____
____	_____	_____	_____	_____
____	_____	_____	_____	_____
____	_____	_____	_____	_____
____	_____	_____	_____	_____
____	_____	_____	_____	_____
____	_____	_____	_____	_____
____	_____	_____	_____	_____
____	_____	_____	_____	_____
____	_____	_____	_____	_____
____	_____	_____	_____	_____
____	_____	_____	_____	_____
____	_____	_____	_____	_____
____	_____	_____	_____	_____
____	_____	_____	_____	_____
____	_____	_____	_____	_____

A child's budget

1. Income — _____ per week from allowance
   _____ per week from jobs
   _____ per week total

2. Percentages — _____ % for tithe
   _____ % for savings
   _____ % for spending
   money

   (Spending money can be budgeted further with an older child.)

3. Account sheets — Keep account sheets for *income, tithe, savings* and *spending*. Use the same category sheets suggested for the family income, but add the child's name and one of the four areas of their budget.

   Since young children have such a small amount in tithe, we had them save it and give it monthly to some area where they could see it being used (i.e., support of a missionary, a special project, Sunday school class, etc.).

A simplified budget - to be used to explain the family budget to children

Some friends shared this budget with their children (ages six, eight, and twelve) to help them understand where the family money goes, what it has been spent on and what they can do to help with expenses. It made it easier for the parents to say "no" and have the children understand.

Beginning salary		$2000
Tithe (and giving)	- 200 =	$1800
House expenses	- 915 =	885
(rent, utilities, insurance, taxes)		
Groceries	- 250 =	635
Clothing	- 150 =	485
Entertainment	- 100 =	385
(includes eating out)		
Babysitting	- 50 =	335
Lessons/sports	- 75 =	260
Life insurance	- 50 =	210
Allowances (earning money)	- 25 =	185
Gifts	- 40 =	145
Household upkeep	- 80 =	65

Sixty-five dollars was left for other expenses including major home purchases (i.e., furniture, new television, etc.), vacations and trips, toys, etc., outside of the normal budget.

The wish list — They listed all the things God had enabled them to do or buy during the last year and thanked Him for His provision. Then they listed the things they would like to do as God provided the money.

Results — The children decided they needed to have a part in the income side of the budget as well as the spending side. They arranged a garage sale to help provide capital. They also offered to wash cars for others. They decided they were old enough to "babysit" themselves by being responsible for their own actions with the oldest girl as the "coordinator" (and official snitch). With their money they took the family out to eat and helped "the budget" with purchases. They began to realize the budget was not "bottom-less" and were motivated to help increase income in order to do some of the things they wanted to do.

Suggested reading
  Giving Yourself Away, Larry O'Nan
  Financial Planning Workbook, Larry Burkett

WORKSHEET FOR CHAPTER 11

Suggested Format for An Update Weekend

1. **Relax.** Take time to enjoy yourselves as a couple. Find a neutral place where you can feel free of everyday concerns and interruptions.
2. **Communicate.** Talk through frustrations, anxieties, concerns. Disarm yourselves from feelings that might get in the way of positive reflection.
3. **Commit.** Trust the Lord in prayer for your time together. Ask for His wisdom in dealing with issues.
4. **Evaluate.** Talk about what has been working well and what has not been working well. Where are the children in working toward their Declaration? What needs to be done next? Where are you in your budget? Are your schedules reflecting your priorities?
5. **Dream.** Envision where you would like to be.
6. **Plan.** How can you get from here to there?
7. **Trust.** Ask God for His strength and perseverance in following through on the plan. Praise Him for who he is and the privilege He has given you of being parents. Describe your child back to the Lord and thank Him for each aspect of the child.

NOTES

Chapter 2

1. John 10:10
2. 1 John 5:13
3. John 10:10
4. 1 Corinthians 14:33
5. Romans 15:13

Chapter 3

1. Mark 12:30-33
2. 1 Samuel 10:23, 16:12; Luke 2:52
3. 1 Corinthians 1:18 — 2:16
4. Proverbs 2:6
5. Proverbs 2:10-12
6. 1 Timothy 3:4-7
7. John 13:35
8. John 3:16
9. Genesis 6:6
10. 1 Timothy 6:10
11. Acts 8:20; Hebrews 13:5
12. Matthew 6:24
13. Luke 10:7
14. Matthew 25:20-30

Chapter 5

1. John 10:10; 1 John 5:11-13
2. 2 Tomothy 2:15
3. Ruth 1:8-14
4. 2 Timothy 2:15
5. 1 Peter 3:15
6. For more information, contact "Walk Through the Bible" Seminars, 1190 Winchester Parkway, Suite 203, Smyrna, GA 30030.
7. Exodus 3:4-22

8. Dennis Rainey, "Train Up a Child in the Way He Should Go," *Worldwide Challenge* (January/February 1985), p. 24.
9. Psalm 119:11
10. Romans 1:20
11. Romans 8:28
12. Proverbs 3:5,6
13. 1 Thessalonians 5:18
14. John 10:10, 5:40; Galatians 5:22,23
15. Psalms 127:3-5, 128:1-4
16. John 14:16 (Living Bible)
17. Hebrews 11:6
18. Galatians 5:16
19. Ephesians 2:3
20. *The Spirit-Filled Life Booklet* (San Bernardino, CA: Campus Crusade for Christ, Inc., 1966).
21. Galatians 5:22,23
22. Psalm 37:4
23. 2 Chronicles 7:14; 1 John 3:22; Matthew 7:7
24. Mark 1:35
25. 1 Corinthians 13:1
26. Hebrews 11:6

Chapter 6
1. 1 John 2:16,17
2. Genesis 1:31
3. Romans 12:1-12
4. Genesis 12
5. Psalm 139:13-16
6. Psalm 139:18
7. Jeremiah 1:5
8. See *A Step Further* by Joni Eareckson (Grand Rapids, MI: Zondervan Publishing House, 1978) for an excellent discussion of working through handicaps.
9. Isaiah 45:9
10. Josh McDowell, *His Image . . . My Image* (San Bernardino, CA: Here's Life Publishers, 1985), p. 37

11. *Webster's New World Dictionary,* D. B. Guralnik and J. H. Friend, editors (New York: The World Publishing Company, 1966).
12. Genesis 1:31
13. Genesis 1:28
14. Genesis 2:24
15. Genesis 2:25

Chapter 7

1. Romans 1:22-32
2. John 17:11
3. 2 Corinthians 9:8
4. Genesis 1:26
5. Bob Biehl, *MasterPlanning Your Life in One Day,* tape cassette series (Laguna Niguel, CA: MasterPlanning Groups International, 1983).
6. John 8:12
7. 1 Peter 3:15
8. *Good News from the Good Earth,* (November 1985), p. 1.
9. Ephesians 4:15; Romans 14:13
10. Romans 14:23; James 4:17
11. Psalms 90:5,6; 103:15

Chapter 8

1. Walter Hooper, *Through Joy and Beyond* (New York: Macmillan Publishing Co., 1982), pp. 97-100.
2. *Webster's New World Dictionary,* D. B. Guralnik and J. H. Friend, editors (New York: The World Publishing Company, 1966).
3. Genesis 2:18
4. Genesis 3:6
5. Ross Campbell, *How to Really Love Your Teenager* (Wheaton, IL: Victor Books, S.C. Publications, Inc., 1982), p.10.
6. Philippians 4:12
7. 1 Corinthians 9:22
8. Joshua 2; 7:16-26

9. 1 Peter 2:17
10. Matthew 18:3-6

Chapter 9

1. Proverbs 23:7
2. Romans 12:1
3. Genesis 1:26
4. Genesis 3:7
5. Genesis 2, 3
6. Psalm 147:3
7. Paul Meier, *Christian Child-Rearing and Personality Development* (Grand Rapids, MI: Baker Book House, 1979), p. 81.
8. Scott Peck, *The Road Less Traveled* (New York: Simon & Schuster, Inc., 1978), p. 81.
9. 1 John 4:19
10. Eugene McDonald, quoted by Meier, *op. cit.,* p. 117.
11. 1 John 4:18
12. Christopher F. Monte, *Beneath the Mask: An Introduction to the Theories of Personality* (New York: Holt Rinehart & Winston, 1980), p. 209.
13. Joshua 4:3-7
14. Philippians 1:1-11; 1 John 1:3
15. Matthew 19:19
16. Peck, *op.cit.,* p. 81.
17. Luke 6:38
18. *Webster's New Collegiate Dictionary* (Springfield, MA: G. & C. Merriam Co., 1979).
19. Proverbs 17:22
20. 1 John 5:11-13

Chapter 10

1. 1 Timothy 6:10
2. 2 Corinthians 9:8
3. Psalms 135:6; 115:3
4. Matthew 26:11
5. Proverbs 10:22 (New International Version)
6. Psalm 71:21

7. Luke 14:28-30
8. Galatians 5:16
9. Matthew 6:33
10. Bill Bright, "We Pray That Our Sons Will Seek First the Kingdom of God," *Worldwide Challenge* (January/ February 1985), p. 15.
11. 1 Corinthians 15:58
12. Luke 10:7
13. Genesis 1:28
14. Matthew 25:26
15. John 16:33
16. Matthew 19:21-26; Luke 12:33-36

Chapter 11

1. Charles Schaefer, "How to Influence Children," *American Baby* (August 1979), p. 32.
2. Ibid.
3. Joyce Maynard, "Bringing Up Moral Children in an Immoral World," *Family Circle* (December 1985), p. 18.
4. Albert Schweitzer, quoted by Steven J. Cole in "Influencing People Spiritually," (Sermon, November 1985).
5. Bruce Narramore, *Help, I'm a Parent* (Grand Rapids, MI: Zondervan Publishing House, 1972), p. 171.
6. Bobb Biehl, *MasterPlanning Your Life in One Day,* tape cassette series (Laguna Niguel, CA: MasterPlanning Groups International, 1983), p.6.
7. Narramore, *Help,* p. 171.
8. Proverbs 16:3 (Amplified Version)
9. Narramore, *Help,* p. 171.

Chapter 12

1. Philippians 4:8,9
2. Psalm 37:7
3. Jeremiah 13:20

RESOURCES

Amplified Bible, The. Grand Rapids, MI: Zondervan Publishing House, 1962.

Joy Wilt Berry. *The Survival Series for Kids.* Fallbrook, CA: Living Skills Press, 1983.

Bobb Biehl. *MasterPlanning Your Life in One Day.* Laguna Niguel, CA: MasterPlanning Groups International, 1983. (For information regarding conferences write: Box 6128, Laguna Niguel, CA.)

Dick Bruso. *Help and Hope for Your Finances.* San Bernardino, CA: Here's Life Publishers, 1985.

John Bunyan. *Pilgrim's Progress.* Chicago: The John C. Winston Company, 1933.

Larry Burkett. *The Financial Planning Workbook.* Chicago: Moody Press, 1982.

Ross Campbell, M.D. *How to Really Love Your Teenager.* Wheaton, IL: Victor Books, S.C. Publications, Inc., 1982.

Campus Crusade for Christ, Inc. *The Four Spiritual Laws.* San Bernardino, CA, 1965.

Campus Crusade for Christ, Inc. *Good News* (an evangelistic tool for children). San Bernardino, CA, 1970.

Campus Crusade for Christ, Inc. *Greatest Treasure* (an evangelistic tool for children). San Bernardino, CA, 1972.

Campus Crusade for Christ, Inc. *Spirit-Filled Life Booklet.* San Bernardino, CA, 1966.

Campus Crusade for Christ, Inc. *Ten Basic Steps to Christian Maturity.* San Bernardino, CA: Here's Life Publishers, 1983.

James Dobson. *Dare to Discipline.* Wheaton, IL: Tyndale House Publishers, 1970.

James Dobson. *Focus on the Family* Film Series (video). Waco, TX: Word Educational Products, 1985.

James Dobson. *Hide or Seek.* (Old Tappan, NJ: Fleming H. Revell, 1974.

James Dobson. *Preparing for Adolescence.* Santa Ana, CA: Vision House Publishers, 1978.

James Dobson. *The Strong Willed Child*. Wheaton, IL: Tyndale House Publishers, 1985, revised.

Fitzhugh Dodson and Paula Teuben. *How to Grandparent*. New York: New American Library, 1981.*

Joni Eareckson (Tada), and Steve Estes. *A Step Further*. Grand Rapids, MI: Zondervan Publishing House, 1978.

Elizabeth Elliot. *Passion and Purity*. Old Tappan, NJ: Fleming H. Revell, 1984.

Adele Faber and Elaine Mazlish. *How to Talk So Kids Will Listen and How to Listen So Kids Will Talk*. New York: Avon Books, 1980.*

Family Ministry. *A Weekend to Remember*. Little Rock, AR. (For information concerning conferences in metropolitan locations write: Family Ministry, P.O. Box 55330, Little Rock, AR 72225.)

Haim G. Ginott. *Between Parent and Child*. New York: Avon Books, Hearst Corporation, 1965.*

Haim G. Ginott. *Between Parent and Teenager*. New York: Avon Books, Hearst Corporation, 1969.*

D. B. Guralnik and J. H. Friend, editors. *Webster's New World Dictionary*, College Edition. New York: The World Publishing Company, 1966.

James and Marti Hefley. *No Time for Tombstones*. Harrisburg, PA: Christian Publications, Inc., 1973.

Howard G. Hendricks. *Heaven Help the Home!* Wheaton, IL: Victor Books, 1973.

Holy Bible, The, King James Version. New York: Oxford University Press, 1917.

Holy Bible, The, New International Version. New York: New York Bible Society International, 1973.

Holy Bible, The, New International Version, Children's Edition. Grand Rapids, MI: Zondervan Bible Publishers, 1982.

Walter Hooper. *Through Joy and Beyond*. New York: MacMillan Publishing Co, 1982.

Gladys Hunt. *Honey for a Child's Heart*. Grand Rapids, MI: Zondervan Publishing House, 1969. (Suggests readings for children.)

Jay Kesler. *Too Big to Spank*. Glendale, CA: Regal Books, G.L. Publications, 1978.

C. S. Lewis. *Chronicles of Narnia*. New York: Collier Books, Macmillan Publishing Co., 1970.

Paul Little. *Know Why You Believe*. Wheaton, IL: Victor Books, 1967.

Living Bible Paraphrased, The. Wheaton, IL: Tyndale House, 1971.

Judith Martin. *Miss Manners' Guide to Rearing Perfect Children*. New York: Penguin Books, 1985.*

Josh McDowell. *Josh McDowell on Self-Image* (tape series). Lubbock, TX: Liberal Tapes, 1983. (For information write: Liberal Tapes, P.O. Box 6044, Lubbock, TX 79413.)

Josh McDowell. *Evidence That Demands a Verdict*. San Bernardino, CA: Here's Life Publishers, 1975.

Josh McDowell. *His Image . . . My Image*. San Bernardino, CA: Here's Life Publishers, 1984.

Josh McDowell. *More Evidence That Demands a Verdict*. San Bernardino, CA: Here's Life Publishers, 1975.

Josh McDowell. *Reasons Skeptics Should Consider Christianity*. San Bernardino, CA: Here's Life Publishers, 1981.

Paul D. Meier, M.D. *Christian Child-Rearing and Personality Development*. Grand Rapids, MI: Baker Book House, 1977.

John T. Molloy. *Dress for Success*. New York: Warner Books, 1975.

Christopher F. Monte. *Beneath the Mask: An Introduction to the Theories of Personality,* Second Edition. New York: Holt, Rinehart & Winston, 1980.*

Bruce Narramore. *Help, I'm a Parent*. Grand Rapids, MI: Zondervan Publishing House, 1972.

New American Standard Bible. New York: World Publishing, 1971.

Larry O'Nan. *Giving Yourself Away*. San Bernardino, CA: Here's Life Publishers, 1984.

M. Scott Peck, M.D. *The Road Less Traveled*. New York: Simon & Schuster, Inc., 1978.

Lorraine Petersen. *Falling Off Cloud Nine and Other High Places* (devotional for teens). Minneapolis, MN: Bethany House Publishers, 1981.

Lorraine Petersen. *If God Loves Me, Why Doesn't My Locker Open?* (devotional for teens). Minneapolis, MN: Bethany House Publishers, 1980.

Lorraine Petersen. *Why Isn't God Giving Cash Prizes?* Minneapolis, MN: Bethany House Publishers, 1982.

J. B. Phillips, editor. *The New Testament in Modern English.* New York: Macmillan Publishing Co., 1952.

John Powell. *The Secret of Staying in Love.* Allen, TX: Argus Communications, 1976.

John Powell. *Why Am I Afraid to Tell You Who I Am?* Allen, TX: Argus Communications, 1969.

Winkie Pratney. *Doorways to Discipleship.* Minneapolis, MN: Provision Books, Bethany Fellowship, Inc., 1975.

Dennis Rainey and Bobb Biehl. *The Questions Book.* Little Rock, AR: Family Ministry, 1985.

Dan Richardson. *Peace Child.* Glendale, CA: Regal Books, 1974.

J. David Schmit. *Graffiti Devotionals for Girls.* Old Tappan, NJ: Fleming H. Revell, 1983.

Charlie W. Shedd. *The Stork Is Dead.* Waco, TX: Word Book Publishers, 1968.

Charles M. Sheldon. *In His Steps.* Old Tappan, NJ: Spire Books, 1985.

John Souter. *Personal Bible Study Notebook,* Volumes 1 and 2. Wheaton, IL: Tyndale House Publishers, 1973.

John and Susan Souter. *Youth Bible Study Notebook.* Wheaton, IL: Tyndale House Publishers, 1977.

James Strong. *The Exhaustive Concordance of the Bible.* New York: Abingdon Press, 1894.

Kenneth N. Taylor. *Almost Twelve.* Wheaton, IL: Tyndale House Publishers, 1968.

Kenneth N. Taylor. *The Bible in Pictures for Little Eyes.* Chicago: Moody Press, 1956.

Joe Temple. *Know Your Child.* Grand Rapids, MI: Baker Book House, 1974.

Merrill C. Tenney. *Pictorial Bible Dictionary*. Grand Rapids, MI: Zondervan Publishing House, 1972.

A. W. Tozer. *The Knowledge of the Holy*. New York: Harper and Row, 1961.

Roger and Donna Vann. *Secrets of a Growing Marriage*. San Bernardino, CA: Here's Life Publishers, 1985.

W. E. Vine. *Expository Dictionary of New Testament Words*. Westwood, NJ: Fleming H. Revell, 1966.

Walk Through the Bible Seminars. 1190 Winchester Parkway, Suite 203, Smyrna, GA 30080.

Joanne Wallace. *Dress With Style*. Old Tappan, NJ: Fleming H. Revell, 1983.

Worldwide Challenge, January/February 1985 issue (special issue on children). San Bernardino, CA: Campus Crusade for Christ.

* We qualify our recommendation of these books in that we personally disagree with them on some issues. However, much of the information they contain is good, and we wanted to include them as resources.